I was honoured when Tom asl  for his new book, "*No Retreat*," and to be honest, I didn't know quite what to expect. I've heard Tom teach on many occasions and know that he is a top notch communicator of truth, but I was totally blown away by this book. As I read, I could hear myself saying over and over again, "*Yep, that's the truth, that's it, no doubt, wonderful, true, that's a fact, and, I like that.*" I loved it! It's an amazing and powerful book about God's true scope and sphere of moving forward that the modern church needs to hear.

Just when you think you've heard and read it all, out comes this book that is really, really great. There is so much wonderful revelation in it that I had to put it down at times and simply reflect on what I was reading. That's just it, truths laid out continually throughout, so much in fact, that I could only read a little at a time. It seemed as if in every paragraph Tom wrote something that was incredibly helpful in understanding the purposes and plans that God has revealed for us, the church, to walk in.

If you're in what we call the five-fold ministry, you need to read this book! If you're not in the five-fold ministry, you need to read this book! So devour it, meditate on it, let it sink in, and then do it again. It's that good! I heartily recommend it to everyone. This book will be a great benefit, not only in terms of pure truth and knowledge, but as an exhortation and encouragement to cause the church to go forward with the shout of, "NO RETREAT! NO RETREAT!"

Pastor Brent Rudoski
Faith Alive Family Church
Saskatoon, Canada

Brent Rudoski
author of *Mercy Triumphs Over Judgment*

Long before I laid my hands on a copy of Tom Trout's marvelous book, I knew it would be life-changing. Over the twenty years that I've known him, hundreds of personal conversations impacted me. Tom's wisdom and biblical revelation have always been astounding. As I read his latest book, *No Retreat*, I found that it is all I imagined. It draws together several of Tom's finest scriptural lessons with profound wisdom and insight. Everybody should pay attention to the unique visions of a father.

J.D. King
author of *Regeneration: A Complete History of Healing in the Christian Church*

I've had the privilege of knowing and walking alongside Tom Trout for the last 24 years. I have been married to his daughter for the last 22 years. Tom has not just been my "father-in-law", he has been an incredibly important spiritual father in my life. He is one of the most consistent, passionate and God fearing men that I know. This book is not just a collection of good ideas he has accumulated through the years, but it is a deep well of experience, study, and God encounters. In these desperate times, God is raising up men like Tom to bring clarity to the body of Christ. The message of individualism and escapism have infiltrated our churches and in doing so, it has created a foundation of shifting sands where we retreat every time we hear the taunt of the enemy. "No Retreat", is a foundational book for all believers that reminds us what it truly means to be a follower of Jesus Christ. If you long to see His Kingdom come and His will be done on the earth, Toms words will be an incredible challenge and encouragement in that pursuit.

Dustin Smith
senior pastor of HopeUC Nashville,
Integrity Music artist and songwriter

NO RETREAT

MOVING FORWARD IN A BACKWARDS WORLD

PASTOR THOMAS TROUT

To all the people who have encouraged me in the Faith and challenged me to write. To all the people that are part of HopeUC/Nashville church that create a community of faith. To pastor Dustin Smith, Here Be Lions ministry and all my family, especially my wife Diana, I want to say thank you for making this work possible.

CONTENTS

INTRODUCTION   1

CHAPTER 1 - A BELIEVER'S PERSPECTIVE   3

CHAPTER 2 - THE CHURCH JESUS IS BUILDING   19

CHAPTER 3 - THE CHURCH COMMUNITY   33

CHAPTER 4 - GOD'S MANDATES FOR LIFE   45

CHAPTER 5 - THE INCREASING KINGDOM   59

CHAPTER 6 - THE KEYS OF THE KINGDOM   79

CHAPTER 7 - REAL WORSHIP   95

CHAPTER 8 - THE POWER OF FAITH   111

CHAPTER 9 - EIGHT STEPS TO THE PROMISED LAND   123

CHAPTER 10 - STEP #1 - MEMBERS & ANOINTED LEADERSHIP   129

CHAPTER 11 - STEP #2 - ORGANIZED HELP TO ADVANCE   145

CHAPTER 12 - STEP #3 - STANDARDS FOR LIFE   157

CHAPTER 13 - STEP #4 - BEING A BLESSING   171

CHAPTER 14 - STEP #5 - TEMPLE TITHING   179

CHAPTER 15 - STEP #6 - HOLY SPIRIT LIGHT   193

CHAPTER 16 - STEP #7 - CELEBRATE THE PASSOVER   205

CHAPTER 17 - STEP#8 - MAKE TWO TRUMPETS   215

CHAPTER 18 - GOD'S PRESENCE CONQUERS   229

INTRODUCTION

This book is an exposition of Scripture from a prophetic perspective. It is meant to encourage, edify, and exhort believers
to live in the fullness of all that God wants for His children on
this earth and at this time in history. It is what I believe the Spirit
of God is saying to encourage the church today.

There is a battle before the body of Christ, but there is also
a great unrealized victory promised. As followers of Jesus we
are promised new life in Christ and given a call and a destiny,
to be lived in fullness by faith, hope, and love.

Christianity is about people and the gospel or the good news.
But this good news is about more than forgiveness of sin and
a heavenly future. It is a gospel of the kingdom of God on
the earth. It is the good news of what Jesus gave his life to
purchase and now empowers his followers to receive and live
by his Spirit.

With this book it is my goal to help all followers of Jesus
recognize the battle, see the way of victory, and then move in

1

faith to conquer and advance, as Israel with Joshua did, into a promised land life fulfilled in the Spirit. God is raising up a people with a voice, a sound of worship, and a call to trumpet throughout the world as His kingdom people, and we want to sound a distinctly clear and loud call for all to see and hear.

CHAPTER 1

A BELIEVER'S PERSPECTIVE

God is good and God has good things planned for those in Christ that worship Him. Most Christians would agree with this statement, if not for any other reason than a belief in the future reward of Heaven for the faithful believer. However, as good as the promise of heaven may be, God wants believers to recognize the many other impressive promises for good that He has given those in Christ. These promises are to be obtained and enjoyed now, right here on this earth. You don't have to wait for Heaven to inherit and live in the goodness of God.

The blessings and promises God wants us to have here in this life, however, won't happen automatically or on their own without our involvement. We can take an example from gardening like Jesus did. In order to have a fruitful and prosperous garden, you not only plant seeds, but you have to water, fertilize, weed, and prune, and you need sunshine. For success, it takes faithful energetic work and effort.

As Christians living in this world there are fleshly habits and worldly thinking that we need to overcome. We are called to love difficult people we live with and work with. We also have to resist the evil spiritual powers who are working contrary to God's desired good for us. And these issues are just part of our life in Christ. Obviously, there is a battle Christians have to fight in order to see more of God's promises unfold in their lives. This is our fight to live in the spiritual promised land of God! In the Bible, God gave the nation of Israel a natural promised land, but when they entered the land, they had to fight to conquer their enemies and live in the land.

THE WAR

We see warrior language throughout the Bible. Jesus said, "Do not suppose that I have come to bring peace to the earth. *I did not come to bring peace, but a sword*" (Matt. 10:34, emphasis mine). The apostle Paul considered himself to be at war in this world when he wrote: "For though we live in the world, we do not wage war as the world does. The weapons we fight with are not the weapons of the world. On the contrary, they have *divine power* to demolish strongholds. We demolish arguments and every pretension that sets itself up against the knowledge of God, and we take captive every thought to make it obedient to Christ" (2 Cor. 10:3–5, emphasis mine). And this means we are at war as well.

Though Paul was talking about a war of words and ideas in these particular verses, there was more to it than just words and thinking. Also included in the Scripture quoted was a reference to *divine power* as an element of this conflict. This means we're talking about a supernatural, as well as a natural, battle. The results of this warfare are as much about life and death as any physical battle, maybe more so, because we are fighting for real life!

We are fighting to enter and conquer a spiritual promised land that is available to every believer today not just in the future. We are fighting to experience more of the presence of God and the fruit of His Spirit in our lives now. We *don't* expect to see the fullness of God's kingdom until Jesus returns, but we *should* expect to see much more that is promised for life in His kingdom here and now. We should expect to see faithful vibrant believers living in community; strong marriages and families; healing and health (both physically and spiritually); prosperity of spirit, soul, and body; strong vibrant churches; powerful corporate worship; and a dynamic growing demonstration of kingdom life in the young and old alike.

THE DEMONSTRATION

This battle reaches into the world as we seek to demonstrate the saving truth of Jesus Christ to the unbelieving all around us.

Paul emphasized the need for preaching the kingdom as he said, "How, then, can they call on the one they have not believed in? And how can they believe in the one of whom they have not heard? And how can they hear without someone *preaching to them?*" (Rom. 10:14, emphasis mine). Certainly, preaching is vital and must happen, but there is more. Peter, on the day of Pentecost, spoke to the people and told them about what Jesus had done as he said, "God has raised this Jesus to life, and we are *all witnesses* of *the fact.* Exalted to the right hand of God, he has received from the Father the promised Holy Spirit and has poured out what you *now see and hear*" (Acts 2:32–33, emphasis mine). Please notice that Peter's appeal wasn't just to the words he spoke, as true as they were, but to a *visible demonstration of power.*

We shouldn't think that preaching is the only means of opening eyes and ears. Those caught in other religions, cults, or atheism already have words and ideas in their mind that they believe. While we are to testify and declare the truth, Christian evangelism isn't only about an argument of words and beliefs, it is also a demonstration of power from the God we serve. The apostle Paul, the one who spoke about preaching also said, "My message and my preaching were not with wise and persuasive words, but with *a demonstration* of the Spirit's power" (1 Cor. 2:4, emphasis mine).

Every living person, regardless of their beliefs, is a demonstration of something. Shouldn't followers of Jesus be a demonstration of His kingdom and its power? Jesus certainly seems to affirm this truth when the disciples of John the Baptist came to question Him as to whether He was the Messiah. Jesus answered their question by pointing to a *demonstration as well as to preaching*. "So he replied to the messengers, 'Go back and report to John what you have *seen and heard*: The blind receive sight, the lame walk, those who have leprosy *are cured, the deaf hear, the dead are raised, and the good news is preached to the poor"* (Luke 7:22, emphasis mine). The battle we fight is something like what Elijah the prophet faced on Mount Carmel with the prophets of Baal. He defeated them with a declaration of truth *and* a demonstration of God's power (see 1 Kings 18).

THE CONTRADICTION

Understandably the idea of fighting a war of any kind is difficult for some people. In many people's minds the idea of war and Christianity, the religion about Jesus and love, are contradictory and don't go together. Many people might even say that the phrase "Christian warfare" is an oxymoron. They assume Christians should always reject war and conflict as contradictions to the ideals of love, forgiveness, and peace. Other people blame many of the world's wars on religion. The truth is that as horrible as war is, it doesn't happen just because of religion. War, both spiritual and natural, happens because of evil working in men in this world.

Another reason Christians might reject the need to battle is they mistakenly connect it to the idea of works. It is certainly true that salvation is not by works. Christ fully paid the price and finished the work of our redemption, restoration, and acceptance into the family of God which we can freely receive, but that's not the end of it. As a type and example look at the nation of Israel in the time of Moses. God set Israel free from Egypt and freely gave them the promised land. But once they were free and entered the land, there was work to be done. Even the Scriptures say, "For we are God's masterpiece. He has created us anew in Christ Jesus, so we can *do the good things* [works] he planned for us long ago" (Eph. 2:10, NLT, emphasis mine), and so it is for us today.

Much of Paul's letter to the Corinthian church is about a conflict that he refers to as war.

When Paul spoke to the church, undoubtedly speaking in love, he was bold and at times confrontational and challenging: "But I will come to you very soon, if the Lord is willing, and then I will find out not only how these arrogant people are talking, but what power they have" (1 Cor. 4:19). Paul loved the church enough to battle for it and confront it with truth. He recognized that for the Christian living in this world, there was a King to be worshipped and honored and also a war to be fought and won.

Today, if there is a concession to Christian warfare, it is generally in terms of intercessory prayer against spiritual forces of evil in the heavenly realms (Ephesians 6:12). Intercession is a crucial and significant part of life and ministry in the kingdom of God. However, Paul also wrote to the church about concerns and conflicts with some of the actual people and leaders living there in the city of Corinth. The fact is that spiritual beings in the heavenly realms were influencing earthly co-conspirators to reject and undermine Paul's ministry. For this Paul had to pray and intercede spiritually while at the same time personally deal with flesh-and-blood people in the church. Paul confronted them about the way they were thinking, what they believed, and how they were living their lives.

Because of his human opposition, Paul's battle was in many ways as earthly as it was heavenly. It was a war in which he was deeply involved and also one which he was determined to win. Paul was fighting for the lives of all believing people and the destiny of the worshipping church.

A BELIEVER'S EXPECTATION

Paul's method of warfare was to pull down the spiritual and mental strongholds of arguments, pretensions, and distortions that were creating disobedience, pride, division, and failure in the church ranks. He used supernatural works of power and divinely inspired words of truth and life. Paul set an example and raised the bar for all of us to follow and we should expect to achieve the same results as we live in victory, honor, and glory to God. The apostle certainly expected to see more from kingdom life in the church than he did, and he was willing to fight for it.

Paul, in his Spirit, knew and saw what was possible in believers and had great expectations for them. He was well aware of the weaknesses of the fleshly nature in carnal man, but he also saw something greater in believing man. He wrote, "But the fruit of the Spirit is love, joy, peace, patience, kindness, goodness, faithfulness, gentleness and self-control. Against such things there is no law. Those who belong to Christ Jesus have crucified the sinful nature with its passions and desires. *Since we live by the Spirit, let us keep in step with the Spirit*" (Gal. 5:22–25, emphasis mine).

Paul didn't expect perfection but neither was he writing just nice ideas or some sort of fanciful suggestions. The letter to the Galatian's was a *divinely inspired word* and the *expectation of God for His church*. We should not flippantly joke about not wanting to have patience or laugh about how we lack self-control or kindness. Paul's words are the promise of God to us and the standard God expects for His people who were filled with the power of His Spirit, which is infinitely greater in power than the miserable power of man's fallen flesh.

In light of this truth, how do Christians today view their spiritual walk and the future of the earth on which they live? What is often the level of expectation in everyday conversation among believers when discussing success, holiness, or Christian victory in life? Isn't it often true that the general focus of most evangelical believers is concern for a saved soul and future home in heaven? At the same time, it's not unusual to hear from Christians a fairly negative world outlook, if not outright fear or hopelessness and even a resigned acceptance, that evil is too powerful and will ultimately overcome just about everything. "What's the use," these Christians might say, concerning the future of the church and this world. Crazy as it seems, many unbelievers often tend to have a more optimistic outlook about the world's future than many Christians have.

The belief in evil growing more and more powerful and taking over till it brings mass destruction on the world is not unusual. In fact, there are those in the church that have taught and promoted some form of this fatalistic future and even promoted it as God's plan. So if the church tends to have a less than victorious mind-set, it's probably the church's own fault.

When it comes to personal lives, many Christians seem to accept their repeated sins, sickness, and typical human weakness, because the thinking goes "we are, after all, just sinners saved by grace." This attitude excuses or promotes godlessness and human failure while offering little hope of a real overcoming power from God in this life. Obviously, Christians slip and sin, but to *expect to continually* sin and fail to obey as *the norm*, is not what Scripture projects for believers.

THE HOPE

The biblical term that speaks of a positive outlook or expectation is *hope*. Hope is defined as "confident expectation." When the Bible speaks of *faith* in the book of Hebrews, hope is key to faith's working. "Now faith is being sure *of what we hope for* and certain of what we do not see" (Heb. 11:1, emphasis mine). Hope is the impetus or strength that drives faith forward. Without hope there is nothing for faith to work with. The Bible also says, "Hope deferred makes the heart sick, but a longing fulfilled is a tree of life" (Pro. 13:12). Denying or putting off hope causes a sickness of heart and lack of faith in anyone. We need strong hope to be a healthy, overcoming people, pleasing to God.

It is crucial to God's kingdom that the hope or expectation level of believers be strong in the Lord. If the church is snared in expectations of failure or futility, it is condemned to stagnate and will fail to move forward. If believers dwell in either a normal expectation of sin or an insulting and paralyzing indifference to the things of God, they will be ineffective in the kingdom of God. Mercy and grace were never intended to be an excuse to quit or resign oneself to defeat. They are the way to a new beginning. So we raise the call and sound the cry to have hope, a great expectation, because of the incredible God we serve.

It's time for the level of hopeful and overcoming expectation to increase in the body of Christ. The kingdom of God must, and absolutely will, overcome fear, hopelessness, and oppressive discouragement through the power of the Holy Spirit and God's Word. The power of evil is *not* greater than the power of the Holy Spirit and Word of God. If hope reigns, faith will conquer, and love will enable His kingdom of life, joy, and power to overcome and advance today.

Hope and expectation grow as the living seeds of God's truth are sown in our hearts. Hope motivates actions that reinforce our words. We need to read, speak, and reinforce the Word of God with our mouths and lives. The church should be a demonstration of confidence in the power of God to overcome evil, changing and empowering people—doing more than just saving us for heaven. The kingdom of God is made of believers who know their God is King and is ruling today.

The New Testament letters vividly describe the spiritual and earthly conflicts of not only Paul but also Peter, John, and other disciples. In spite of many situations that could have caused them to lose hope, they fought to overcome struggles, both internal and external, in churches and in themselves. Some churches were divided and struggling over power, position, gifts, authority, doctrine, and especially faith. Paul faced opponents promoting evil, unbelief, divisions, and an elitist party spirit. They distorted the truth and appealed to people's selfish flesh and religious pride. Yet Paul refused to be crushed or destroyed (2 Cor. 4:8–9)

At Corinth the rampant strife, jealousy, and disregard for the true worship and spiritual welfare of fellow believers placed that church in a situation that allowed both physical and spiritual weakness, sickness, and even death (1 Cor. 11:30). Despite facing these obstacles, Paul's goal was to have a community of people worshipping, living in victory, and displaying to a dark, lost world the goodness and glory of God. Paul's expectation level remained high and full of faith regardless of what he was having to deal with.

The apostle fought this war because he envisioned a group of true believers able to walk both individually and corporately by faith. These believers would live to worship together and receive the full promises of a covenant God. The church Jesus is building will overcome the world. It will be a unified group of believing people living in covenant, in community, in faith, and in love, while it functions supernaturally and prospers in every way as the Lord's representative on this earth. His church is a people living kingdom life in a spiritual promised land with God.

Our goal as the church today should be the same as Paul's goal for the church then. Though many are being added to church membership lists and there are efforts at ecumenical unity and interfaith charitable works, many church members today are still wandering in biblical ignorance or confusion with lives void of real spiritual empowerment. Too often you can see, in both leaders and church members, the same fleshly insecurity and carnal weakness struggling for power and recognition that Paul confronted. Not only that, but this kind of behavior is producing the very same kind of weakness, sickness, failure, and death that plagued the Corinthian church.

There is hope, however, because God has a plan to enable believers to overcome self-centered carnality and hopelessness, win their war, and become the church He desires. The spirits behind the opponents of Paul have not changed and they still have the same agenda today as they did in his day. If they are still operating the same way, with the same agenda, then it is certainly time for the church to wake up and not be fooled by its enemy any more (2 Cor. 2:11). The carnal and weak humanistic ways of thinking and living in this world can and will be overcome by the powerful living God. It is time for Christians, followers of Jesus, to reach maturity and demonstrate to the world the true glory and overcoming presence of God.

Kingdom life is the presence of God producing the fruit of Himself in the assembled body of Christ. The presence of God is more than just routinely saying, "God is in the house." It is real and tangible. It is seen and demonstrated in vibrant worship, life, and miracles. God's presence is His Holy Spirit touching, healing, and transforming people in every way until they are truly conformed to the image of Christ and living as a visible example of the kingdom of God on this earth. This kingdom life won't be our perfection, but it will be a demonstration of spiritually empowered and mature believers.

It might be a new revelation to some, but we must understand that Jesus is not planning on coming and rescuing a weak and sick church from some huge earthly calamity. The tribulation that Jesus said we would have in this world was not about our destruction or our defeat but is simply the struggles and opposition in this world that we must overcome by his strength. God's plan is to empower a kingdom of people that will overcome its struggles in this world by loving and glorifying Him. He's going to have a people prepared and ready to be the church to which Christ can return and over which Christ will rule in power and glory forever.

It is often a shock for believers to hear, for the first time, the biblical truth that they will not spend all eternity in heaven. Heaven is real and for the redeemed, but according to the Bible the redeemed will come back to earth with the Lord to receive resurrection bodies and then inhabit a new earth with a new heaven. The life we live today is preparation for the future new earth coming after heaven! Heaven is not the promised land! The promised land for believers is supposed to be happening today. It is a victorious life in and with Christ. It is a truly transformed corporate community of believers enjoying the presence of God, serving Him and each other, and walking in the love of the Lord Jesus Christ.

Not only does God have good planned for His people in Christ, He also has a plan of battle and victory, and this book is about that plan. In Scripture we have an example of promised land struggles in Israel. As we study the example of Israel in the promised land we can learn how to live a promised land life today. God expects us to worship in Spirit and truth, to hear the voice of the Lord, win the war against all enemies, and live a kingdom life, all while preparing the way for the Lord and His kingdom's fullness.

CHAPTER 2

THE CHURCH
JESUS IS BUILDING

We need to look at the church in God's kingdom and see God's vision. The church is *the one and only thing that Jesus declared he would build* (Matt. 16:18), and it's at the heart and center of the purpose and revelation of Jesus Christ. It's crucial that we know what Jesus gave His life for and what He desires, if we are to know our purpose and destiny.

Obviously there have been problems with the church. Jesus speaks to the church at Laodicea in his revelation to the apostle John:

I know your deeds, that you are neither cold nor hot. I wish you were either one or the other! So, because you are lukewarm—neither hot nor cold—I am about to spit you out of my mouth. You say, "I am rich; I have acquired wealth and do not need a thing." But you do not realize that you are wretched, pitiful, poor, blind and naked. I counsel you to buy from me gold refined in the fire, so you can become rich; and white clothes to wear, so you can cover your shameful nakedness; and salve to put on your eyes, so you can see. (Revelation 3:15–18)

These words are from one letter that's part of a group of letters from the Lord to seven different churches all existing in John's day. All but one of those churches, according to their letters, needed correction and all needed and received encouragement to strengthen and help them. This particular church is one that suffered from a collection of issues including spiritual blindness; lukewarm hearts; haughty attitudes; and a faithless, passionless existence that threatened to bring about its very ejection from the presence of God. That's a terrible prognosis for any church.

It's worth noticing that there is a stark and dramatic difference between the Laodicean church that John describes and another church of Roman Asia, the church of Ephesus that the apostle Paul describes in an earlier letter. Paul wrote to the Ephesian church and its leadership to help them know how to become the church that Jesus was building:

Now these are the gifts Christ gave to the church: the apostles, the prophets, the evangelists, and the pastors and teachers. Their responsibility is to equip God's people to do his work and *build up the church*, the body of Christ. This *will continue until* we *all come to such unity* in our faith and knowledge of God's Son that *we will be mature* in the Lord, *measuring up* to the *full and complete standard* of Christ. Then we will *no longer be immature* like children. We *won't be tossed and blown about* by every wind of new teaching. We *will not be influenced when people try to trick us with lies* so clever they sound like the truth. Instead, *we will speak the truth in love, growing in every way more and more like Christ*, who is the head of *his body, the church*. He makes the whole body fit together perfectly. *As each part* does its own special work, it helps the other parts grow, *so that the whole body is healthy and growing and full of love.* (Ephesians 4:11–16, NLT, emphasis mine)

There are some that might go so far as to say that this Ephesian letter is depicting a future, eternal and perfected church that only comes with the return of Christ. They see a beautiful picture of the spiritual fullness of the New Testament church in Christ, but not something to actually be expected before Jesus returns. However, we need to point out that God promises this church, in its faith, unity, and maturity, the ability to overcome trickery and waves of bad teaching. We certainly don't expect trickery and bad teaching to be present in Heaven or the future earthly kingdom of Christ. No, Paul was not describing some perfected heavenly church from the future. This letter is a vision of what the apostle believed Christians and the church were capable of, and would become on earth now, with the power of God's Holy Spirit. We are expected to fight for this kind of church on earth now.

Then, at the same time, the Laodicean church that John wrote to in the Revelation is interpreted by some to be a prophetic picture showing the condition of the typical church in the last age of history. These commentators teach that each of the seven churches of John's Revelation represents one of seven different church ages that would be seen in the future after John's time. I see no biblical basis for this thinking. These ideas are merely suppositions and figurative interpretations, but what *is* clear is that all seven of those churches existed in the time of John. What is also obvious is that all had their strengths and weaknesses and all needed instructions and encouragement. Significantly, that's not unlike the church everywhere today.

A CHURCH VISION

An argument could easily be made from some perspectives that the church today would seem to be prospering and doing well. For example, there are more professing followers of Jesus

Christ today than at any other time in history. We have mega-churches with multimillion-dollar facilities and all kinds of church related ministries offering help of every conceivable flavor. There are untold numbers of evangelistic and outreach ministries all over the world. The Christian marketing industry is flourishing as it produces and sells a seemingly endless variety of items for the Christian consumer, more things than one can imagine. Also, there is the growing Christian media world of music, TV networks, radio stations, movie production, books, magazines, blogs, and much more. By some standards, it appears that God's church is doing very well, and for this we should certainly thank God.

However, God does not tell us to evaluate ourselves based on our own observations. The church needs to listen to God's evaluation and learn what it is that He desires. This was part of God's criticism in John's letter to Laodicea: "You say, 'I am rich; I have acquired wealth and do not need a thing.' But you do not realize that you are wretched, pitiful, poor, blind and naked" (Rev. 3:17). Then, in the same way, Paul wrote to the church of Corinth and challenged their lack of wisdom in comparing themselves with themselves when he said, "We do not dare to classify or compare ourselves with some who commend themselves. When they measure themselves by themselves and compare themselves with themselves, they are not wise" (2 Cor. 10:12).

The only valid appraisal of the church and its' success is the opinion of Jesus. In Jesus' Revelation to John, Jesus wanted to come in and be present in the church. In Revelation 3:20 Jesus is standing and knocking at the door of the church, looking for someone to open the door so he could come in and dine with them. The truth is, the church had shut the door on Jesus. The church was literally prohibiting the presence of God in their assembly.

The fact that this happened then is why the church today needs to evaluate itself in light of God's standard and expectations. We need to ask if the church today falls short in this biblical example. Does the church today foster such community that there is no need among its people? Are the sick being healed, the dead being raised, the lepers being cleansed, and demons being driven out as Jesus commanded in Matthew 10:8? This is the kind of thing that Jesus and His disciples did when he was ministering on the earth. However, it is the kind of thing some religious leaders now say ended with the last apostle, whoever that might have been, and isn't supposed to be part of the church's ministry today.

The truth is, powerless religion has a way of twisting theology and Scripture to its own benefit while excusing itself for its spiritual shortcomings. While some religious leaders today make excuses, there seems to be as much disease, divorce, and character failure in the church as there is in the world of unbelief. This poor testimony of God's faithfulness and power convinces unbelievers that they are right in their unbelief and rejection of Jesus.

The lack of visible supernatural and miraculous workings of God in His church lessens genuine changed and empowered lives. Believers are supposed to experience the kind of dynamic and spiritual transformation that produces passionate, vibrant, and excited worshippers and enthusiastic, faithful servants of God. People should be able to live in community and enjoy the prosperity of God and not be overcome or consumed by anything other than the Spirit of God.

Shouldn't Christians exude an obvious abiding spiritual presence and power that makes them different, as they live dedicated and victoriously prosperous lives as true followers of Christ? Likewise, shouldn't we also be a people that courageously faces trials and tribulations, persevering in faith and being boldly willing to die if necessary? Could it be that in the mind of Jesus the church today needs to open the door of its corporate heart and seek fervently more of His tangible presence?

Scripture says the Lord is actually looking for a people who will worship Him in Spirit and truth (John 4:23). Believers must be willing to fight the indifference and casualness that creeps into the church. We must battle to worship and live in the ever-increasing supernatural presence and power of God.

NEW PRIORITIES

To fulfill God's vision for the church, our priorities must change. The Laodiceans were living by standards that encouraged a defeated and lukewarm church. A church caught in dead religion is motivated by human priorities rather than God's priorities. Human priorities center on man's needs or preferences rather than the need to honor God and seek His will first. Dead religion also emphasizes the individual and their personal needs and desires over the community and its relationship with God in a corporate life in Christ.

In the typical church in America today many different messages are being promoted. Some preachers spend time focused on the individual sins of people and the need to repent, while others proclaim feel-good messages to lift the people's spirits. Still others explain how to save souls for Heaven, and of course there are those teaching about relationships and family. Also, we shouldn't ignore the politically motivated messages of some pulpits. All of these concerns are valid and need to be dealt with, but they miss the even greater problems that should be concerning the church today, which are not really knowing God's first priority or being aware of His presence and power.

It's possible for the church to focus on the many physical needs of its' people and forget the deeper spiritual condition, which actually are the primary cause of all our issues. So, even with the many varieties of messages that predominate the church today, the people can still shrivel spiritually and fail to develop the spiritual muscles they need. It's very possible to attend a church and not know how to actively and passionately worship and experience the presence of God. It's possible to sit in the pews every Sunday and not know God's powerful and tangible corporate love, nor be part of His empowered and anointed body, God's supernatural community of healing.

Compounding these problems is the truth that the church, despite the amount of biblical scholarship and versions of the Bible that are readily available today, still remains biblically ignorant. Much of today's church has spiritual teeth that are rotting out from the sugar milk messages it consumes each week. It is much like what Paul said to the Corinthians, "Brothers, I could not address you as people who live by the Spirit but as people who are still worldly—mere infants in Christ. I *gave you milk*, not solid food, for you were not yet ready for it. Indeed, you are still not ready. You are still worldly. For since there is jealousy and quarreling among you, are you not worldly? Are you not acting *like mere humans?*" (1 Cor. 3:1–3, NIV, emphasis mine).

Those Corinthian believers weren't able to chew the meat of God's Word, and so couldn't become the mature and strong disciples Paul desired for the church. They were caught in their own selfish world and were either ignorant of the truth or rejecting it and living as "mere" humans rather than becoming scripturally trained and spiritually empowered disciples of Jesus Christ.

THE WAR IS REAL

For the church to succeed it must come to grips with the truth that it is in a life and death war, and its priorities need to be examined and maybe changed. A war is happening in our world, both inside and outside the church. A war not only with spiritual but physical enemies. While the Christian church is unwittingly fighting against itself and defeating itself, there are radical, disciplined religious groups in this world whose goal is world subjugation and domination. They are so devoted to their god they are willing to blow themselves to oblivion for their cause. They are fully willing to sacrifice everything they have, including their lives to achieve their goals. They endorse and actively promote killing their enemies and allow no room for compromise or discussion, only total capitulation. These zealous groups have no interest in sharing this world with any other religion; their only goal is total annihilation or conversion of everyone.

The church has to recognize there is a very real war happening. When Paul said, "though we live in the world, *we do not wage war* as the world does" (2 Cor. 10:3, emphasis mine), he wasn't saying we *don't* have to fight a war at all, nor was he invalidating certain principles of war that all armies, whether natural or spiritual, must follow. We are in a war and if an army is to win, it must know its objectives. Once it knows what it is to do, it must also have good leadership, and it must follow that leadership without rebellion, dissension, or division. Armies don't win by taking votes, listening to every soldier's opinion or by every soldier trying to be his own leader. Members of an army have to put self-interests aside, get in position, follow orders, and seek the group objective if it is going to conquer the enemy.

Even with the many Christian denominations and their various doctrinal statements and differences, there are still core essentials most Christians generally agree on about sin and death and salvation. Most Christians know they are forgiven and have access to heaven when they die; they also know they should live righteous, moral, and charitable lives as much as possible. While knowing these points is good and reason to thank God, it is still only a starting point. It is essential for Christians to realize that Jesus purchased much more than Heaven and morality for the believer.

A more comprehensive understanding of biblical salvation recognizes the spiritual conflict and the awesome promised land life confronting the believer. Knowing about the Christian battle helps us to understand and recognize the goal of Christ for us on the earth. The Bible states that Christ came to destroy the work of the enemy, the devil (1 John 3:8). The devil's work was to break up the relationship between man and God and creation and God. Jesus then came to restore creation to God the Father and man's relationship with God, both now and in the future.

We must fully comprehend what Christ achieved if we are

to understand salvation. What Jesus did was actually begin the restoration process for all of creation, both heaven and earth, as well as all the cosmos, to the glory for which it was created. The greater work of Christ was to actually inaugurate and demonstrate the kingdom of God.

Jesus won the war on the cross. The battle happening now is one for kingdom expression, expansion, and ultimate fulfillment. The fullness of the kingdom is the pinnacle of salvation for mankind. John wrote, "Then I heard a loud voice in heaven say: "Now have come *the salvation and the power and the kingdom of our God*, and the authority of his Christ" (Rev. 12:10, emphasis mine). John was acknowledging both the victory Christ won at the cross and the ongoing work of His rule. Looking to the future work and mission of the body Jesus said, "You have *made them to be a kingdom* and priests to serve our God, and *they will reign on the earth*" (Rev. 5:10, emphasis mine). What John recorded connects the purpose and fulfillment of Christ's victory with the responsibility of the body of Christ to respond and fulfill Christ's purpose in the earth.

John writes, " 'Let us rejoice and be glad and give him glory! For the wedding of the Lamb has come, and his bride has made herself ready. Fine linen, bright and clean, was given her to wear.' (Fine linen stands for the righteous acts of the saints)" (Rev. 19:7–8). Please note the important phrase "his bride has made herself ready." John is talking about the visible fruit of a response on the part of the bride of Christ, the church. He wasn't talking about the church waiting for something to happen to it or for it. John indicated the church should know and respond to what had already happened.

In these verses John connects the kingdom reign of God and its ultimate fulfillment to the bride, the church of Jesus Christ, *making herself ready*, meaning believers have to respond to the Word and do what God asks of them. The kingdom of God is to be demonstrated in a group of people who are given over to the rule of God in their lives. However, the effect they have on the surrounding world as they freely demonstrate the power of God's kingdom will be contested by a defeated enemy who does not want to relinquish his evil power over them. This is the battle we fight—to see the fulfillment of God's plan for the church Jesus is building and the kingdom of God.

CHAPTER 3

THE CHURCH COMMUNITY

Because of the predominant focus in our culture on individuality and personal rights, many believers come into the church with a similar individualistic mind-set and purpose. For example some may join because they're told it is the right thing to do, it'll be good for them. Church is seen as a way of enhancing their own personal lives. They can find help with their own personal problems.

This thinking is understandable because everyone has issues in life. The problem with looking to the church as simply the answer to individual needs is that the focus is all about the individual. When people see themselves as "Lone Ranger" Christians, they fail to see the larger corporate picture that God blesses. God wants a servant community, a corporate body, or an army working and serving together as a unit. The unit's purpose being the welfare, growth, and victory of the entire group as well as the individual members.

A GROUP THING

Because of our culture's individualistic mind-set, many believers
don't understand that God looks at His followers as a group as
much as, if not more than, individuals. Certainly, Jesus appeals
to the individual to come to Him, but He then puts the individual in a family, a community, a servant army of believers. It is
imperative that Christians realize how much Christ personally
identifies with this group as His corporate representative body
and army in this world.

When Saul was on his way to Damascus to pursue followers
of Jesus "He fell to the ground and heard a voice say to him,
'Saul, Saul, why do you persecute me?' 'Who are you, Lord?'
Saul asked. 'I am Jesus, whom you are persecuting,' he replied."
(Acts 9:4–5). If you ask yourself who Saul had been persecuting,
the answer of course was the church. In this light Jesus reveals
that this was the same as persecuting Jesus Himself.

Jesus spoke this way because He personally identifies with
this group called the church. The bottom line is that if you
hurt the church, especially the corporate group, then you hurt
Jesus. Being part of a corporate identity tends to be a foreign
concept for the individualistic-minded western believer. We
don't realize how badly isolated Christians fracture and defeat
the church. The old saying "united we stand and divided we
fall" has spiritual ramifications for the church. Jesus even said,
"Any kingdom divided against itself will be ruined, and a house

divided against itself will fall" (Luke 11:17). This is absolute truth from the Lord Himself.

Americans and other Western-minded believers tend to gain their identity through their own achievements and careers. Whereas the Eastern mind-set recognizes that identity more readily comes through a corporate relationship to family and community. We must recognize that the Bible is first of all an Eastern book written initially to Eastern people who understood or thought with the mind-set of a group identity. If we want to understand and appropriately apply Paul's words to the church, then we will have to learn to think with a Corinthian culture or Eastern mind-set. We have to read the Scriptures not only in their own context but also in the context of their group culture and history.

The Bible states, "The one who is in *you* is *greater* than the one who is in the world" (1 John 4:4). The "you" here is plural not singular, and the comparison is between the church corporate versus the world and the spirit of antichrist that is in the world. Paul also asked the Corinthians, "Don't you know that you yourselves are God's temple and that God's Spirit lives in you?" (1 Cor. 3:1). When Paul wrote, "you yourselves" he was speaking of a group or corporate concept of the church as the dwelling place of God's Spirit. This is our primary purpose in the earth today, to be the temple, the worshipping church, the warring army, and the kingdom dwelling place of the greater

One in us all together.

Being the successful warring and worshiping church will happen only as we learn God's way of life and community. We need to see ourselves today through the eyes of Christ, so we can be the church He intends to build. The church Jesus is building will prevail against the powers of evil and win the spiritual war confronting it. The only way to win, however, is to wage war not just as individuals but as a corporate body of believers. It is the corporate body alone that God empowers and has mandated. Of course the church needs strong individuals who are victorious in life on a personal level. However, it needs even more to succeed and function as a corporate body, a true spiritual force in our world. We, the church, have a responsibility to learn and promote this way of life today. The bible reinforces the need for the body to help strengthen itself when it says, "From him the whole body, joined and held together by every supporting ligament, grows and *builds itself up* in love, as *each part does its work.*" (Ephesians 4:16)

God's followers have been given instructions for life as a church. There is an order to what the church needs to do and how it is to do it. For example, God has given us a way of worship that pleases Him and that He will accept. Evidently not all worship is acceptable (Heb. 12:28). The grace of God is more than just a covering of our sins, it is an enabling power that gives us the means to worship God acceptably. With God's grace we can have the presence of God with us and win the war we face both individually and corporately.

THE NUMBERS EXAMPLE

In the Old Testament book of Numbers there are a series of commands God gave Moses, the leader of Israel, for how they were to handle certain situations. Remember that Israel is an example to us for how to achieve the promises of God as a covenant people of God. These commands were intended to establish within the people of Israel certain procedures that demonstrated their faith. Their wholehearted response was necessary for the entire group's move into the promised land, which God wanted them to conquer and then dwell there prosperously.

By studying these commands and applying them to life issues today, the church can overcome their enemy. God's way, if it is honored, will enable the church to worship in the presence of God, win its war over its enemies, and move into the kingdom life God has promised it. In the following chapters we will consider and study the types or patterns found in these commands.

The Bible teaches us about a life in Christ for today that is as different from the lukewarm sub-biblical Christianity of Laodicea as the promised land life of Israel was different from the Sinai desert back then. By following God's prescribed way and moving together in the Spirit and worshiping Christ in community, we can overcome the ways of the world, our selfish desires, and false religion. When we follow God's way as a church, we become His glory in this earth. As the church grows into the fullness of Christ and worships and lives the life ordained by God, it will truly be the blessing it was called and created to be, having an ever-increasing impact on everyone and everything around it

THE HOLY SPIRIT LIFE

There is a powerfully vital and fulfilling life for the believer to live in the Holy Spirit. To help our understanding we need to ask ourselves what part does the cross of Christ play in our lives. Was the cross the end and final work for us or was it the beginning of our life's work? Christianity will rightly say that Jesus was victorious and accomplished everything on the cross and the work of salvation is finished. There's even a popular worship song that says, "the cross has the final word." What's often *not* said is that while the work of atonement— propitiation, redemption, and justification— was finished on the cross, all this work was just a doorway for us to be acceptable to God. It is the way to enter into His presence, into a new relationship, and to receive all His promises and become His anointed corporate body.

The cross opened the way for the continuing and ongoing work of Christ, which is the outpouring of His Holy Spirit on all flesh to enable the building of His church. There is work to be done by the redeemed body of Christ to advance and finish establishing the kingdom. Christ's sacrifice was only the beginning of what God intended to do for mankind.

The Spirit empowers the "good works" which Christ has prepared for us (Eph. 2:10). Christ's work of making us acceptable, allows us to draw near to God and worship Him freely, but Christianity is much more than just being forgiven and acceptable. In God's presence He will anoint us, fill us, equip us, grow us, and transform us. He actually transforms us into godly and spiritually fruitful people. Because of everything He has done and is doing, we have a divine responsibility to fulfill our destiny as His children, His church, on this earth.

Our destiny and calling is to be people who actually display the fruit of the Spirit (Gal. 6) and live a life that demonstrates the power of His love in us (1 Cor. 13). The Salvation Christ paid for will not only transform us individually, it enables us to be His victorious, empowered church that is filled with the Holy Spirit. This empowered body has work to complete before Jesus can return here to earth (Acts 3:21). Paul said, "The God of peace will soon crush Satan under your feet" (Rom. 16:20). While this text is not about the complete eradication of evil in this world, it is about an overcoming church crushing the enemy by the power of the Holy Spirit living in it.

Romans 16:20 is about the kingdom of God being empowered to invade the ranks of the enemy and win the war. Hell is not destined to win or overcome God's church. Scripture says, "I will build my church, and the gates of Hades [hell] will not overcome it [not prove stronger than it]" (Matt. 16:18). We are called to put God's enemies under our feet by expanding His kingdom in us and throughout the earth. This will be accomplished by learning by God's grace obedience to the Lord in the power of His Spirit and by discipling the nations and bringing them to worship God.

The way to gain disciples is to live your life in such a way that it causes others to desire to know the God we worship and serve. This happens as we live with the spiritual intimacy and success in life and ministry that Christ intended and paid for us to have. Christ has promised us *abundant living* in love, hope, joy, peace, thanksgiving, all through the power of the Spirit so that we can be a witness to the world around us. To facilitate this demonstration we need the increasing manifest presence of God in His church and its worship of Him.

THE ISRAEL EXAMPLE

Israel, after leaving the slavery of Egypt, camped at Mt. Sinai and then proceeded to wander aimlessly in the wilderness. After wandering in the wilderness because of their lack of faith and obedience, Israel was eventually allowed to enter into the promised land. In the same way the church needs to cease wandering in its own wilderness. The church's wilderness is its passionless worship, spiritual immaturity, theological confusion, self-sufficient spiritual attitude, worldly distractions, and lukewarm indifference to God. God is calling the church to come out of this wilderness so it can enter into its' own promised land, where the body of Christ enjoys the victorious life in Him.

According to the Bible, the things that happened to Israel in the wilderness were written down for the church as an example. The apostle Paul wrote to the Corinthians: "Now these things occurred as examples to keep us from setting our hearts on evil things as they did. . . . These things happened to them as examples and were written down as warnings for us, *on whom the fulfillment of the ages has come*" (1 Cor. 10:6, 11). He wrote to the Romans and said, "For everything that was written in the past was written to teach us, so that through endurance and the encouragement of the scriptures we might have hope" (Rom. 15:4).

The Bible amply records the events experienced by Israel as they moved through the wilderness and prepared to enter and live in the promised land. Studying and learning from Israel's example will give us direction and hope for living the kind of life which Christ paid for. This is *not* about some legalistic application of God's law for believers, but it is about understanding the spiritual principles and patterns that God chooses to use with His people and how His kingdom operates in this world. The apostle Paul said that we can learn and apply the principles from Israel's past because we live in what he called the "culmination of the ages" (1 Cor. 10:11).

In Corinthians 10:11 we see the English word *examples*, which can also be translated *type*. Looking at Israel as a "type" of church, it is fair to compare their journey in the past from Egypt to Mount Sinai and finally to the promised land to the journey of the church today. For example, believers today come out of a type of Egypt, which was their slavery to sin, a life of unbelief and a destiny of judgment and death. They then begin a faith journey of growth and transformation much like the wilderness time of Israel. Learning how to know and walk with God, they may stumble, get lost, or wonder about as they find their way. But as they continue, they find themselves growing in faith and beginning to mature as His followers.

The last step of Israel's journey was the promised land. However, Israel's promised land is not to be equated as a figurative type of Heaven for the Christian. Thinking of Heaven as the promised land does not make any sense. You don't have to fight for or conquer Heaven. You are welcomed there as a believer upon death. But in our world today the believer must fight and overcome the world if the kingdom is to increase and covenant promises are to be received. The promised land was a place on earth and for the Christian today, the promised land is our life in Christ lived here and now in this world. Like Israel had to conquer its enemies to occupy the promised land that God had given them, the church must also go to war to receive the promises of God in their life today. The goal of this book is to make the body of Christ more aware of the war they must fight and hopefully help prepare them to more successfully carry it out today.

OUR PROMISED GOAL

Promised land living is kingdom life. It is the destiny and goal of the church here on earth. Kingdom life is abiding in the Lord's presence, being filled with His Spirit, and overcoming the spirit of the world and flesh. It's having His Holy Spirit rule in us until we truly reflect His glory and honor. The corporate church will increasingly conform to the image of Christ as it truly and acceptably worships God. Then God's kingdom will spread into all the earth. It is the churches destiny to press forward and fill the earth with His glory, as we overcome his enemies and fulfill the purpose God has for us.

Paul wrote to the Ephesian church:

Finally, be strong in the Lord and in his mighty power. Put on the full armor of God so that you can take your stand against the devil's schemes. For our struggle is not against flesh and blood, but against the rulers, against the authorities, against the powers of this dark world and against the spiritual forces of evil in the heavenly realms. Therefore put on the full armor of God, so that when the day of evil comes, you may be able to stand your ground, and after you have done everything, to stand. (Ephesians 6:10–13)

Paul understood the goal and the war the church was engaged in. The apostle also expected the church to faithfully battle and actually overcome its opposition. The question today is do we know and expect the same thing?

CHAPTER 4

GOD'S MANDATES FOR LIFE

The kingdom life and its expansion starts with a mandate. If you look up the definition of *mandate*, you'll find several variations, but basically it means "an authorization to take action as a legitimate representative." For example, Adam was given authorization by the Lord to act here on earth as His legal representative.

Also a mandate, along with being authorization to act as a legal representative, is "a command to be obeyed and not just a suggestion or good idea." God has commanded His people to action and expects them to comply. With this in mind it is important to realize that the "representative" we're speaking of is the corporate church and not just individual persons. While individual believers are to represent Christ while on the earth it is not to the degree of the mandate that has been given to the

4646

464646464646

collective corporate body of Christ.

We will consider two major mandates recorded in the Bible—one in the Old Testament and the other in the New Testament—in order to understand how these mandates apply to us, the people of God today. Although these two mandates are different in their wording, they both offer great promise and hope while at the same time placing the responsibility on God's earthly representatives to respond and carry out His commands.

THE FIRST MANDATE

The first mandate recorded in scripture is in the first book of the Bible:

> So God created man in his own image, in the image of God he created him; male and female he created them. God blessed them and said to them, "Be fruitful and increase in number; *fill the earth and subdue it*. Rule over the fish of the sea and the birds of the air and over every living creature that moves on the ground. (Genesis 1:27–28, emphasis mine)

This is labeled the Dominion Mandate by many Bible commentators. It is the command of God the Creator to Adam and Eve, all his creation, and all who would follow Adam and Eve as their children and heirs.

Basically the intent was for Adam and Eve to care for and

expand the garden until it covered the earth and their children filled it. God blessed or favored them and wanted them to "be fruitful, multiply greatly, fill to fullness the earth and subdue it" That command to them was a mandate to do several things. One in particular was to bring the earth into submission, dominate it, tread down enemy opposition, and keep it under their authority. God expected man to dominate over the fish of the sea, birds of the sky, and over every living thing that creeps on the earth. The mention of creeping things is probably a prophetic reference not just to snakes but to the chief serpent, the devil himself.

God is omniscient. He knew the enemies man was going to face, and yet He said rule over them and have authority over them. The words *subdue* and *conquer* are aggressive, conquering words. God used this kind of combat terminology because he knew that Adam was going to have a battle to face. His words were prophetic since man had not yet fallen, but an all-knowing God could see the future and knew there was conflict and a fall coming. He knew temptation was coming and that Satan, the devil, was going to be the chief instigator and adversary.

One of the orders God gave Adam concerned the Tree of the Knowledge of Good and Evil:

"The LORD God took the man and put him in the Garden of Eden to work it and take care of it. And the Lord God commanded the man, "You are free to eat from any tree in the garden; but you must not eat from the tree of the knowledge of good and evil, for when you eat of it you will surely die." (Genesis 2:15–17)

God's mandate was given to Adam and Eve, but they failed to accomplish its demands and honor God's trust in them.

The Bible states, "When the woman saw that the fruit of the tree was good for food and pleasing to the eye, and also desirable for gaining wisdom, she took some and ate it. She also gave some to her husband, who was with her, and he ate it" (Gen. 3:6). Adam actually failed in more than one way, but he most obviously and disastrously failed when he, knowing the command of God, went ahead and took the fruit from Eve and ate of it. He knew the command of God but went along with her anyway and therefore he, Adam, was responsible for the failure. Adam also dishonored and doubted the goodness and faithfulness of God. This broke their relationship with God.

Let me suggest an idea of how this story could have gone differently. What might have happened if Adam had been faithful to his mandate as the man of God under the authority of God? If he had respected God's authority and obeyed Him, it might have looked like this:

When Eve was tempted by the devil and gave in and ate the fruit of the tree and offered Adam the forbidden fruit,

Adam would have said, "Eve I can't do that. My God and my Creator has said I can't eat that fruit. I won't follow you. I cannot do it Eve. To disobey would be dishonoring to God and His word to us." After this Adam would have sought for God and humbly approached Him instead of hiding from Him. Adam would then have said, "Father, Eve has committed a grievous sin. She has disobeyed your word and eaten that which was forbidden her. She was taken in by deception and temptation and failed to honor and glorify you. But Father I ask you to forgive Eve. If someone has to die because of this sin, Father, let it be me. Take me Adam, your delegated representative, and let me give my life. I will die for Eve so that she might live."

GOD'S WAY

If Adam had resisted the fruit, everything would have been different. God might have taken Adam's life, but since he didn't actually sin, he couldn't have died and would have been raised back to life. Mankind coming from Adam would have been righteous through him. Of course, it didn't happen like that. But to the glory of God, Jesus, the "last Adam," did do things according to His Father's will and therefore conquered death and redeemed all those who believe.

Since the fall of Adam much has happened to advance the kingdom of God. Jesus overcame all sin at the cross and is extending His victory now! We don't always consider as we should the fact that while Jesus conquered He is even *now still conquering* in us and through us and we, the church, have become His instrument. Remember the little verse stating, "The God of peace will soon crush Satan under your feet" (Rom. 16:20). Well we, the church, are the feet. It is always His power, but we are the instrument of God's victory and glory in this earth.

The idea of crushing Satan will seem foreign for those who think that living as a Christian is mostly about just hanging on to your faith until He comes. Living in the kingdom has never been about hanging on until the end, because it is about a victorious and overcoming people fulfilling their destiny in Christ as His church. This is what the power of God working in us and through us is meant to accomplish to the glory of God. Paul explained it well when he wrote: "For he must reign until he has put all his enemies under his feet" (1 Cor. 15:25). He is not coming back until the enemy is overcome by His feet. The return of Jesus is based on an overcoming church. He isn't returning to be enthroned in all fullness and glory until the enemy is defeated under His feet!

The good news is that because of Christ the church, the body of Christ, is overcoming evil on the earth. The church must raise its level of expectation for itself. If it wants to please the Lord or achieve His purposes, the church shouldn't settle for activities the world deems acceptable. What Christ purchased is a congregation of believers that the transforming presence of God inhabits and is transforming into a powerful witness of light and life overcoming a dark world.

The church that Jesus is building will be an international body of fervent and spiritually connected members, a community with an all-consuming and passionate love for God and each other. They will be a people serving and enjoying the Lord with all their hearts. It will be an assembled, mature body, anointed by the Spirit of God, infused with the supernatural power of God and instructed by the Word of God. This church, operating in the delegated authority of God and having God's grace and His Spirit forcefully working together, will accomplish seemingly impossible things as the kingdom of God on the earth.

This is the kind of church that will be an answer to the prayer the Lord taught his disciples to pray that said, "your kingdom come, your will be done on earth as it is in heaven" (Matt. 6:10). This church will also be an answer to the prayer Jesus prayed: "I have given them the glory that you gave me, that they may be one as we are one—I in them and you in me—so that they may be brought to complete unity. Then the world will know that you sent me and have loved them even as you have loved me" (John 17:22–23, NIV). Why would we doubt that Jesus would get answers to His prayers? His prayer will be answered, and we can be part of that answer.

THE SECOND MANDATE

The second mandate we need to consider will help us see how the enemy can be placed under the feet of the church. This second mandate is recorded in Matthew 28:18 and is generally called the Great Commission: "Therefore go and make disciples of all nations, baptizing them in the name of the Father and of the Son and of the Holy Spirit, and teaching them to obey everything I have commanded you. And surely I am with you always, to the very end of the age" (Matt. 28:19–20). The command in Matthew is actually the same basic mandate as Genesis 1:27–28. This second mandate or commission is just couched in terminology that has been understood to have a different emphasis. The promise in Matthew of His being with the disciples is not without condition. The implied condition is, I will always be with you all the time *while you are doing what I have asked you to do*. Many miss not only the implications of the condition but also complete understanding of the command.

Just before Jesus gave that command, He said, "All authority in heaven and on earth has been given to me (Matt. 28:18). The word he used for *authority* is *azuzia*, which means "power of rule". God the Father gave Jesus the right and authority to rule and have dominion in the earth. He is not to stand back and let evil run rampant and unchallenged through this world. Jesus has legitimate power and authority over the powers of darkness. Evil authority will bow, bend, yield and buckle to the righteous authority and power of Jesus. Evil has to yield to Him and His righteousness and always will. The Lord said, all authority had been given to Him in heaven and on earth. It was true then, and it is still true today that as we act as His delegated authority on this earth according to His mandate, we can walk in His powerful life.

In the same way that the command of God to Adam was to have dominion over the earth, the command of Jesus to the disciples was to bring the world of people under the full dominion of His kingdom rule. But when reading the command or mandate many don't actually hear what Jesus said. When reading the words of Jesus, people tend to unconsciously interpret them somewhat as follows: Go therefore and make some converts from among the nations. We must recognize that's not what He said. What he said was, "Go and make disciples of *all* nations" or in other words, "Go and make the nations my disciples."

We don't want to suggest Jesus was saying every single solitary individual was to be a disciple nor that we are to change everything in the world and make it totally transformed. That change will only happen with the return of Jesus himself. I suggest, however, that there is a far larger scope to the command than is typically understood. The goal is the general discipling of the nations. We must think bigger. He was saying in effect, "You disciples, go and you make every nation on the face of the earth as much of a believing, disciplined Christian nation as possible." When the power of God changes enough people and they live as true disciples of Jesus, then they will influence and change the world around them.

THE OPPOSITION

Christianity has an adversary, an enemy that opposes the kingdom of God. He manifests his efforts in many ways but one of those ways is false religion. Within false religion there are zealots following false gods that are out to overcome Christianity. However, they are not trying to just make a few disciples among the nations. Their plan is to convert or subjugate entire nations and the entire world is their goal. These zealots are thinking in bold terms of spiritual invasion. Now is certainly not the time for Christians to shrink back or hesitate in the face of opposition?

Jesus already commanded His followers to change all the nations as much as possible into faithful, believing, obedient followers of Christ. That is obviously a bigger task than just going and making "saved" converts among other people groups. Missionaries need to think in terms of expanding and establishing His kingdom on earth. This expansion is about changing the character of cultures and the nature of societies. The church must think on a much longer and larger scale. We have to think in terms of planting kingdom Life with an eye to the future all over the world. If you ask how is that possible? You just limited God, and you just limited yourself. You aren't seeing the larger vision of what God wants to do with His world.

Weak theology and poor eschatology (belief about the end times) have created doubt and questions about the power of God. There are Christians today who live like their old nature is more powerful than the Spirit of God that is in them. Other believers seem to have been persuaded that the devil has more power than God. These weak and unbiblical ways of thinking all need to be changed!

Christians must stop following the patterns of this world and start thinking according to the patterns of the Lord Jesus Himself. If believers will actually seek to be transformed, allow the Lord to change their attitudes, and work hard and worship zealously, they will become a blessing in the earth like Abraham was promised: "and all peoples on earth will be blessed through you" (Gen. 12:3). The greatest fulfillment of this promise is of course the coming of Christ as the seed of Abraham and Savior of mankind. However, it was never the intention of God that the work of Christ be limited in any way.

THE PLAN FULFILLED

The natural extension and blessing of Christ's initial coming and victorious work at Calvary is for people to be filled with the Holy Spirit and become totally transformed. As believers are changed, the kingdom grows and thereby becomes a blessing to all the people and nations of the earth. Every time a believer says yes to God or His Word and no to sin or temptation, they are taking back ground from the enemy. Saying yes to God is the clearest picture of releasing the kingdom and its authority while effectively binding the enemy and his ability to work in the earth. As more and more people believe, the kingdom will increase and have the ability to eventually touch or affect every nation and aspect of society in the world.

God wants the kingdom message delivered with power into the entire world so that the world will acknowledge Jesus as King and Lord. His goal, like He said to Adam, is for us to be fruitful and multiply or reproduce disciples. A disciple is a trained, faithful, anointed, empowered, and obedient servant. The world is the field, and the people are the harvest, new creation beings living to glorify, worship and serve the one true living God. Jesus died to purchase all the nations of the world so he could come down and live in a new world here on this earth.

God's ultimate goal isn't to get Christians into Heaven; it is to finally bring Heaven down to a new earth:

> Then I saw a "*new heaven* and a *new earth*," for the first heaven and the first earth had passed away, and there was no longer any sea. I saw the Holy City, the new Jerusalem, *coming down* out of heaven from God, prepared as a bride

beautifully dressed for her husband. And I heard a loud voice from the throne saying, "Look! God's *dwelling place is now among the people, and he will dwell with them.* They will be his people, and God himself will be with them and be their God." (Revelation 21:1–3, NIV, emphasis mine)

Peter makes reference to this same idea when he wrote: "But in keeping with his promise we are looking forward to a *new heaven* and a *new earth*, where righteousness dwells" (2 Pet. 3:13, NIV, emphasis mine).

Christians and churches must be careful that they don't become so heavenly oriented that they ignore or forsake what is to happen to the earth. God isn't going to throw this earth away. He's going to restore or renew it. It is here, on a new earth, that God the Father will finally be glorified and be worshipped by all nations and all living creatures. The dominion mandates will finally and ultimately be fulfilled, the war won, and the true promised land (the whole world) conquered.

CHAPTER 5

THE INCREASING KINGDOM

The kingdom of God, in the simplest of terms, is the King ruling over all His domain of the created universe. The church is a part of that domain as well as an example of His kingdom rule on the earth. Jesus said of God's kingdom rule: "The coming of the kingdom of God is not something that can be observed, nor will people say, 'Here it is,' or 'There it is,' because the *kingdom of God is in your midst*." (Luke 17:20–21, NIV, emphasis mine). Jesus was speaking of the internal presence of the Spirit and God's dominion happening in His followers.

God has given believers His Word to lead them into a Christ-honoring way of life. As followers of Jesus live their lives in Him and He lives through them, they demonstrate His kingdom reign both individually and as a group. Disciples that demonstrate lives submitted to God and to each other, loving and honoring each other as they work to serve the Lord, are a demonstration of the kingdom to everyone around them.

When Luke talked about the coming of the kingdom of God, he wasn't talking about a government on the earth at that time. Neither was he contradicting the belief in an eventual earthly rule by Christ as a literal, physical King on earth. He was talking about a future kingdom.

When the Lord talked about His kingdom he didn't mean when enough believers organize and amass enough votes to win elections to force changes in the law that coincide with biblical law or ethics. This is not to say that Christians shouldn't vote their consciences; they should. But don't confuse being a responsible citizen of whatever country you live in and exercising whatever civic freedoms you have with the way that God will build His kingdom. The Medieval Church Crusades to conquer the Holy Land were a sad example of what happens when humanity tries to establish the kingdom of God by human dominion and coercive force.

KINGDOM GROWTH

Isaiah the prophet gave us a beautiful promise of kingdom growth when he prophesied about the kingdom of Jesus:

> Of the *increase of his government* and *peace* there will be no end. He will reign on David's throne and over his kingdom,

establishing and upholding it with justice and righteousness from that time on and forever. The zeal of the LORD Almighty will accomplish this. (Isaiah 9:7, emphasis mine)

Notice a couple of things here. First the rule of the King will have no end. The second thing is that peace will be the ceasing of war and rebellion of man against God and will also have no end. It's talking about man living in harmony with God. The verse is not referring to a world free of war between men.

The work of Jesus on earth illustrated the rule of God's kingdom in man. The kingdom of God is established and grows as individuals change how they think and live their lives by being conformed to Christ. The cumulative effect of spiritually transformed people on their surroundings creates a changed atmosphere spiritually, socially, economically, and politically. People operating under the kingship of Jesus don't need the written laws of man to dictate the way of righteous living and behavior; it comes as an outworking of the Spirit's work in them and a writing of God's Word and law on their hearts.

It is not possible for the kingdom to develop and grow without the needed work of converting and discipling unbelieving humanity. Attempts to try and bring about kingdom life and community by legislating civil laws based on biblical law and Christian expectations of moral behavior are doomed to fail. Just and appropriate laws are needed in society, and

Christians should be a part of formulating and enacting those laws. However, creating a theocracy or trying to establish Christian values on unbelieving people legislatively isn't how God will establish His kingdom.

What God wants is for people to come to Him on their own, be transformed in their own hearts, and then live in such a way as to influence others to make godly choices. As more people are transformed, taught the Word of God, and live by the Spirit, society and culture will be impacted and transformed. Then God's kingdom will invade more and more of the world. This is the pattern God gave Israel as they came into the promised land: "Little by little I will drive them out before you, until you have increased enough to take possession of the land" (Ex. 23:30). This incremental and progressive change is an organic type of transformation. It is true kingdom growth empowered by the Holy Spirit.

KINGDOM GOAL

The kingdom of God is demonstrated by people following the Lord Jesus Christ not just as a Savior but as Ruler and King and enjoying the benefits of life under His authority and in His presence. A kingdom, after all, is really all about the king. The goal and purpose of God's kingdom today is for there to be a people who love and obey the King and are passionate about restoring the glory and honor of the King on the earth. The kingdom of God must never be relegated to a purely future event since this restoring work of kingdom people actually happens now.

Though there are many kingdom objectives, the Bible indicates that the foremost kingdom goal is to restore the honor and glory that belong to God (1 Tim. 1:17; Rev. 4:9, 11). In the beginning of time, Satan and Adam denied God the honor and glory He rightfully deserved by rebelling against Him. Adam was the only creature to be created in the image of God, a high honor. So when Adam questioned God's goodness and right-eousness, it was the greatest dishonor and insult to a holy, loving, righteous and good God. He was dishonored and disgraced by His very own creation made in His own image.

Now, by the grace of God we have the greatest honor and privilege given to us. We are redeemed, born of His Spirit, able once again to give God the Father the glory and honor that are rightly His. As His people we are to trust God, believe Him, and embrace His rule in our hearts and lives as we live with a purpose of bringing honor to Him and His kingdom. As people bought with Christ's blood, we not only have the honor, but we have a responsibility to respond and serve Him (1 Cor. 6:20).

Ultimately and finally, as believers, we are corporately to be presented as the kingdom to the Father by Jesus as the fulfill-ment of His mission: "Then the end will come, when he hands over the kingdom to God the Father after he has destroyed all dominion, authority and power. For he must reign until he has put all his enemies under his feet" (1 Cor. 15:24–25, NIV). We will fight and we will win the war for His honor and glory.

KINGDOM SHREWDNESS

For God's enemies to be trodden underfoot the people of God must have a change of heart and spiritual goals. They must become wise or shrewd in the ways of the covenant kingdom of God. "I am sending you out like sheep among wolves. Therefore be as shrewd as snakes and as innocent as doves" (Matt. 10:16). We need to be wise in the ways of God as well as our enemies' ways.

Some would doubt the idea of the kingdom being able to overcome the great flow of evil in our world. They see many awful things as part of God's judgment on wicked people. But Jesus pretty much challenged this idea when he corrected his disciples as he healed a blind man. When they assumed the blindness was a judgment caused by sin Jesus corrected them (John 9:2–7). The horrific things that happen in our world are not so much God's judgment because of evil, as much as they are the result of this world struggling with itself as it's filled with fallen and evil people.

We need to be understanding and act shrewdly. The things happening in our world today are largely because of men sowing evil and reaping evil, or it's just the result of living where evil is real and wants to rule. This fallen world still operates by the spiritual principles that God established before the fall of man; it is the order of a fallen creation. We need to remember that the sin of man was judged at the cross of Christ. What God is more actively concerned with now is the unbelief, rebellion, and dishonorable hearts in the lives of believers who are created to be better.

God's actions and movements today are generally centered on, and in response to, believing covenant people as they pray and seek to fulfill the commission of God and disciple the nations. God is focused on believers and their prayers more than on the world's sinful ways, as horrible as they may be. God is just and will ultimately execute justice on the world's wicked. But we should be aware that the wicked of the world are already judged and destined to death and hell, but their punishment will come later. Everything happening now is to provide the opportunity for people to repent and be redeemed. Without a doubt there will be a time of final judgment and justice, but that time is not until the work of the church is accomplished first. Many people cry out today like the saints of Revelation: "They called out in a loud voice, "How long, Sovereign Lord, holy and true, until you judge the inhabitants of the earth and avenge our blood?" (Rev. 6:10, NIV). But they were told they had to wait; there was more to be accomplished.

Since the beginning of the church age there have been

questions concerning the kingdom of God and how it was to be fleshed out in the lives of believers. Jesus said clearly, "For the people of this world are more shrewd in dealing with their own kind than are the people of the light" (Luke 16:8). Believers must come to understand and have insight into how the covenant kingdom of God operates and the goals to be achieved. In this text Jesus was saying that believers must be as shrewd and wise in living and functioning in the kingdom as the people of the world are in living and operating in the world. As believers today we can't just sit back, put our feet up, and do nothing while naively assuming everything will just work itself out and we'll be protected from problems and tribulation.

KINGDOM PROSPERITY

One area of life that the church must gain wisdom about is prosperity. Shrewd people of the world have no problem doing business in this world with the expectation of prospering and increasing their wealth. A major deception in Christianity is the false religious concept that equates poverty with greater spirituality. We are certainly supposed to grow spiritually, but we don't have to do so at the sake of material wealth.

Something that will help us in the realm of handling worldly goods and doing business is to understand that the word *profit* is not an evil word or something that is contrary to living a godly life. Profit is the gain you achieve after expenses are paid, or it is the increase on your investment. God created man with the desire and need to profit. The farmer doesn't plant seed without expecting a harvest. A builder doesn't invest time, energy, and resources in building without expecting a finished structure. This is how the creation grows, and it is something God established and put in man. It is not evil.

Jesus appealed to the profit motive when He said, "For what will it *profit* a man if he gains the whole world, and *loses* his own soul?" (Mark 8:36, NKJV, emphasis mine). Jesus was clearly appealing to the inborn desire in man to profit or gain and do well as He appealed to them to gain their salvation. He didn't deny the powerful motivation that God had placed in man nor did He call it evil. He recognized it as a means to accomplish His goal in the earth, and He used it for good.

The very idea that gaining wealth or doing anything with the goal of profitability would somehow diminish a person's spirituality is absolutely contrary to kingdom life and growth. To vilify the desire for material success as evil and carnal while at the same time promoting poverty as a means to spiritual development is perverted and just wrong. There is no place in the Bible where poverty is equated with superior spirituality. In fact, poverty is called a curse (see Deut. 28:45–48).

Another subtle twist of thinking concerning wealth has to do with charitable giving. Some people say, "we don't give to get." Why does this appeal to Christians? Because there is a false unspoken ideal called altruism. Altruism is the idea of giving or sharing without any expectation of getting something in return, and it appeals to human pride. It is easy to think you are a better person or more righteous if you give with no desire to get anything in return.

The idea used to support this thinking is that you only want to be a blessing and aren't looking to be blessed. The truth is that when you give, you always get something in return, even if it is just a good feeling. And it's alright to expect this. Both thinking that you shouldn't want anything in return or that you are somehow a better person to give without expecting anything are absolutely contrary to the way of God's kingdom. God Himself gave His son in order to get a harvest of people. Sowing and reaping is a kingdom principle that was instituted by God. The Lord didn't sow without any desire to reap. So why would we make the mistake of trying to be more righteous or better than God Himself? This is merely a work of the enemy to deceive and a trick God's people in order to defeat them.

Rejecting prosperity or material goods out of a fear of being less spiritual is not the way to achieve spirituality. We are supposed to be shrewd in the ways of God. Jesus says, "You cannot *serve* both God and money" (Luke 16:13, emphasis mine), it does not say you can't *have* both God and money. Just because some have a propensity to be greedy doesn't mean all Christians should avoid doing business and being prosperous.

Scripture says that "the wealth of the sinner is stored up for the righteous" (Pro. 13:22, NKJV).

It also isn't evil to have the desire to prosper. In fact, believers should expect to prosper and learn to be good stewards of the goods they acquire as they sow expecting a return. God gives His people understanding so they can learn to be shrewd and wise and stop being foolish and easily defeated. Believers should use wealth and material goods for good and shouldn't let material goods capture and control them. Material wealth is a tool essential to the operation of God's world and is intended to be used for the good of the kingdom.

Believers wanting to advance the kingdom have to stop looking at material prosperity as somehow in opposition to their spiritual goals. We must learn that kingdom life is a life prospering in *every* way. Every believer needs to ask God, who freely gives, to help them change. We have to repent of any false religious pride that equates poverty with being more spiritual or as a means to spiritual growth or maturity.

There is a very real and practical need in the body of Christ for prosperity of all kinds and for the money to do the work of the ministry and to win this war. The church is self-defeating when it is reluctant to teach prosperity or encourage tithing and giving as a way of life and achieving blessing in God's kingdom economic system. The church should be a center of entrepreneurial initiative and possess a strong work ethic that produces wealth for the kingdom. How else can we be a blessing to those in need, not to mention the nations of the world?

Paul corrected similar false thinking in the church in Colossae when he wrote:

> Since you died with Christ to the elemental spiritual forces of this world, why, as though you still belonged to the world, do you submit to its rules: "Do not handle! Do not taste! Do not touch!"? These rules, which have to do with things that are all destined to perish with use, because they are based on human commands and teachings. Such regulations indeed have an appearance of wisdom, with their self-imposed worship, their false humility and their harsh treatment of the body, but they lack any value in restraining sensual indulgence. (Colossians 2:20–23, NIV)

Austerity and deprivation of worldly goods or prosperity in any form does not increase spiritual capacity. Rather, true spirituality overcomes being controlled by material goods and freely uses them for godly purposes as well as enjoyment.

Certainly, as a godly believer we can't be greedy, envious, or jealous, but at the same time we should not lack the ability to prosper so we can support the purposes of the kingdom.

As Christians we are to operate in the realm of the natural world as well as the realm of the supernatural. We may not be "of the world," but we certainly can learn to be wise and shrewd and operate "in the world" in order to promote the kingdom message and life. To be one-sided when it comes to the natural or the spiritual is to be severely limited in our capacity to fight the war we are called to win. In fact, if the church fails to win this battle to operate in both the spiritual and the natural world, the church will be without resources and defeated.

KINGDOM LOVE

We can't talk about the kingdom of God without talking about the love of God. The kingdom of God is obviously about love, since the Bible says that "God is love" (1 John 4:8, NIV). Jesus commands us to " 'Love the Lord your God with all your heart and with all your soul and with all your strength and with all your mind'; and, 'Love your neighbor as yourself' " (Luke 10:27).

One of the most well-known verses of scripture is "For this is how God loved the world: He gave his one and only Son, so that everyone who believes in him will not perish but have eternal life" (John 3:16, NLT). Even many nonbelievers can quote John 3:16, although they don't understand the depth of what is being said.

The problem we sometimes have with the word "love", especially the love of God, is that we confuse human feelings or emotions of affection that we call love, with God's righteous actions that define love. For example, we tend to think of loving someone based on our emotions of affection or passion for them. Whereas God's love was demonstrated without regard to affection or approval.

John was quoting Jesus as He talked about how God, in goodness and righteousness, acted in response to the need of man for His help and redemption. Many people tend to read John 3:16 as though it is talking about *the amount* of affection God had for sinners rather than correctly reading it as a description of *the manner* of how God reached out to help mankind and the cost involved for this help. God's action was motivated by His inherent righteousness, goodness, and justice—unlike fickle human emotions of affection.

Another passage points out our dependence on God to even love: *"We love, because He first loved us.* If someone says, "I love God," and hates his brother, he is a liar; for the one who does not love his brother whom he has seen, cannot love God whom he has not seen. And this commandment we have from Him, that the one who loves God should love his brother also" (1 John 4:19–21, NASB, emphasis mine).

Some people might read verse 19 as though it is describing a reasonable cognitive response on our part to the love of God. A better understanding is that John is talking about our enablement, or the ability that's given to us by God's acting on our behalf in Christ. Because of what Christ did we can now love like He loves. The text says, "we love," and if you put it in context with verse 20, which talks about loving God, then the reasonable understanding is that we can now love God first and love others as well because of what God has done for us in Christ. We are now empowered to choose and act like God would act towards others without being limited to an emotional motivation.

As noted earlier, the bible says God is love. "God is love. Whoever lives in love lives in God, and God in him." (1 John 4:16b, NIV). The great truth is that for us to love is to be godlike in our behavior towards others. Godlike love really has nothing to do with our human emotions, affections or approval, but it has everything to do with being filled with the Spirit of God and acting with the righteous and good nature of God and being like Him. As human beings it is perfectly reasonable to desire and exhibit emotions of affection, passion and desire, but we can't confuse these with godly love.

Godly love is a kingdom work. He loves us and we love Him, and we are called to love each other through Him. We are to minister in love, which is a key to His anointing and power working through us. God's love is reflected in caring, helping and serving the needs of others. His love is a selfless and sacrificial action, without any kind of a self-serving focus on human feelings of warmth and comfort. Emotional, passionate love and affection, as desirable and pleasant as they are, are not the same as godly love in Christ, though they may be the fruit of godly love's demonstration.

The Bible says, "This is love for God: to obey his commands. And his commands are not burdensome" (1 John 5:3, NIV). We stated that God's love isn't really about warm fuzzy feelings. It isn't about liking someone and having affection and approval toward them, though it is possible that could happen. Enjoyable feelings are attractive to the flesh, but they lack the strength and power to overcome flesh, sin, and the world. It is always wonderful to enjoy heartfelt expressions of caring love and affection, but you can't walk onto the battlefield armed with warm, fuzzy feelings and expect to defeat the enemy. You must go into war equipped with godly weapons and armor. You need to be ready for war, or you're going to be defeated. Biblical, agape love is about acting or responding in righteous goodness and obedience to God. It is motivated by commitment, faithfulness, and holy passion for doing the will of God with zeal.

KINGDOM SOLDIERS

The apostle Paul instructed Timothy how to prepare for the spiritual war and the hardships he might encounter in life and ministry. Paul knew circumstances could cause even a soldier to wander from his duty and objective. The way to be a good soldier is to stay strong in the grace of the Lord and keep focused on the goals and truth of the kingdom while instilling them in others. This is why God gave the following commands through Paul, to Timothy:

You then, my son, be strong in the grace that is in Christ Jesus. And the things you have heard me say in the presence of many witnesses entrust to reliable men who will also be qualified to teach others. Join me in suffering, like a good soldier of Christ Jesus. No one serving as a soldier gets involved in civilian affairs—he wants to please his commanding officer. (2 Timothy 2:1–4, NIV)

Paul's first exhortation for Timothy was to be strong in the Grace that is in Jesus. Typically, grace has been defined simply as the "unmerited favor" of God. While this definition is true, it falls short of fully describing God's favor toward us. It is more accurate to define grace as the favor of God that gives enabling spiritual power to accomplish God's purposes. We are to be strengthened with the enablement of the Spirit that comes by the grace of being in Christ Jesus.

Paul wanted Timothy to use this enabling grace and take the instructions he had given him and transmit and entrust them to reliable and faithful men who would in turn be enabled and qualified to teach others also. This meant he was to develop anointed and dependable men who would, in turn, also train disciples and equip warriors for the war. Paul called Timothy to endure his share of hardships and suffering like a good, first-class soldier of Jesus Christ.

It usually doesn't take believers long to discover that the Christian life isn't always a bed of roses, and that there are battles to be fought. Paul says that no soldier worth his salt gets entangled in civilian life. Paul is not saying you can't have a business or enjoy life and also be a Christian, which would be ridiculous and destructive to the kingdom and its prosperity. Not being entangled simply means that you aren't caught up or led by or taken captive by civilian issues. It means staying free to follow the Lord at all times.

We live and operate in the world, but it isn't to be our guiding priority or purpose. For example, many people move all over the world in order to take a better job and earn a bigger salary. For many who consider relocating, often their first priority is their careers or income. While this is certainly understandable, a kingdom-minded person would first consider where God wants them to serve or be connected. It's right to ask the question "Will this job actually help the kingdom of God?" There is a difference between the call to serve and the call of career. Let your mind be set like flint that we do all things for the glory of God. God can and does use jobs and careers to facilitate His kingdom; we just need to keep first things first.

God will bless and anoint us to win this battle. The church is the chief expression of God's kingdom presently in this world. It's our opportunity to faithfully receive the kingdom's power, grace, prosperity and love that is available to operate among and within us. The church must remember that the gospel is the good news of the kingdom. God has given His kingdom the commission and authority to overcome this world. The good soldier always keeps his purpose and target first in his attention and actions because the kingdom of God is always about advancing and increasing.

CHAPTER 6

THE KEYS OF THE KINGDOM

We've talked about the church; we've talked about the kingdom of God; and now we will look at the kingdom way. Jesus makes a powerful statement to Peter and the disciples. He declares to them, "I will *give you the keys of the kingdom* of heaven; whatever you bind on earth will be bound in heaven, and whatever you loose on earth will be loosed in heaven" (Matt. 16:19, emphasis mine).

We don't really need any more understanding of this phrase than to recognize what a key is and what it does. Keys are something that can be used to lock or unlock. This means that keys have the ability to either allow or restrict access. The keys, in this case, enable us to change and affect how things in our world and the kingdom of God happen. Scripture uses the words *binding* and *loosing* to indicate they can either hinder, limit, or restrain on one hand or free, release, or enable on the other.

In the following chapters we will consider several "keys" of the kingdom of God. He has given His church keys to use to advance the kingdom thus unlocking the glory of God. We are going to look at some of those keys and how to use them.

HONOR AND AUTHORITY KEYS

Two primary and essential key qualities to serving God and increasing the kingdom are honor and authority. The kingdom of God only operates and succeeds in an *atmosphere* of honor and from a *position* of authority. Of course, for any kingdom to be good it needs a good king, which we have in Jesus. But a good king can only do so much for his subjects, they have to respond and do their part. This is why a kingdom functions and succeeds based on the level of honor and authority its subjects give to the king.

The Scriptures command the church to have a heart that gives honor to whom honor is due (Rom. 13:7). What Paul was talking about was an attitude. Honor starts with a heart attitude, and what God is after is a heart quick to give honor to others. Too much of the time we are quick to challenge authority and fail to respect their opinion, while at the same time injecting our own ideas into the equation. The Lord places a high value on the giving of honor.

Possibly one reason God values honor so highly is because

of Adam's betrayal, in the garden of Eden (Gen. 3). Adam and Eve's questioning of God's Word was more than just rebellion, it was a blatant disrespect and dishonoring of both God and His authority. Adam and Eve's attitude of dishonor had a terrible and lasting impact on the creation. That is why giving honor where honor is due is such a significant key to kingdom life and victory.

To honor the Lord also means to honor those He has established in positions of authority over you. The letter to the Roman church speaks directly to this issue:

> Everyone must submit himself to the governing authorities, for there is no authority except that which God has established. The authorities that exist have been established by God. Consequently, he who rebels against the authority is rebelling against what God has instituted, and those who do so will bring judgment on themselves. (Romans 13:1–2, NIV).

Notice how God identifies with those who represent Him, even if they aren't good representatives.

It is understandably difficult to honor or treat respectfully people you may strongly disagree with or even dislike. Their character may not be what it should, or they may have any number of qualities that make it challenging to honor them. For example, to honor a governing official who is not doing an

honorable job or whose work may even be harmful or corrupt
can seem impossible.

My father served in the army in WWII. One time I asked
him how he could salute officers that he thought weren't doing
a good job or were creating hazardous situations for his friends.
My dad said that he didn't salute a man; he was saluting the
uniform and what it represented. The commanding officers'
uniform represented the Army he vowed to serve and the country
he was defending. You see men are weak and fall short in many
ways, but maintaining discipline and honoring authority keeps
the army from chaos. We can always have an attitude of honor
in our hearts toward God and trust Him to help us regardless
of the people involved.

Rebelling against authority puts you at odds with God
because it is ultimately a rejection and dishonoring of God
Himself. It is behaving like Adam. Some people might think
that it is alright to ignore or disobey those authorities if they
make mistakes or abuse their power. This is not true. Honor
is not to be given on the basis of someone's performance, it is
given unto the Lord and to honor God who created us all and
raises up or brings low (Ps. 75:7) and will judge all.

Rules and laws that seem unjust or wrong to us cannot be
selectively ignored. If people started to choose which laws they
should or should not obey, we would have chaos and destruction. God is a God of order and not of chaos (1 Cor. 14:33). If

there are bad laws or rules, then we need to be responsible and work to change them not just ignore or violate them. Also, to expect authorities to never make a mistake would be placing an impossible standard on them. There are righteous ways for us to respond to wrong being done by those in authority, but outright rebellion or blatant acts of dishonor aren't God's way.

In the church today, and especially in the Western culture, there is a serious problem with people's attitude toward authority. We have a culture that exalts independence, personal rights, self-rule and doing whatever they want to do. However, believers place themselves in direct conflict with God and in a position of defeat when they are dishonorable and don't respect authority. God requires a standard of honor for authority in His church today.

DISHONOR LIMITS

The word *honor* means "to have high regard so as to esteem, to recognize or to value."

Jesus shared a major insight in the Scriptures about this kind of honor. He was in his hometown of Nazareth, teaching in the synagogue on the Sabbath when those listening to Him became upset:

When the Sabbath came, he began to teach in the synagogue, and many who heard him were amazed. "Where did this man get these things?" they asked. "What's this wisdom that has been given him that he even does miracles! Isn't this the carpenter? Isn't this Mary's son and the brother of James, Joseph, Judas and Simon? Aren't his sisters here with us?" And they took offense at him. Jesus said to them, *"Only in his hometown, among his relatives and in his own house is a prophet without honor."* He could not do any miracles there, except lay his hands on a few sick people and heal them. And he was amazed at their lack of faith. Then Jesus went around teaching from village to village. (Mark 6:2–6, NIV, emphasis mine)

Jesus was not honored in His own hometown. There was certainly no lessening of anointing or power with Jesus himself, He was the same, but there was a *limiting* of what He was able to do for those people in His hometown. As they chose to treat Him as someone common, not worthy of their honor, they lost the capacity to receive blessings from Him. They surrendered the opportunity to experience the fullness of all He could have done for them. Their familiarity toward Jesus led to a lack of reverence and honor, which robbed the town of experiencing the greatest Jesus had to offer. The text says that Jesus was amazed at their lack of faith.

Because they lacked faith the Scripture says that he could only heal a few sick people but could do no miracles there. The implication is clear that he possibly would have not only healed the sick among them but also would have done miracles as well. It is important to see that in the case of those in Nazareth, their *lack of faith or trust was caused by a failure to give honor* to Jesus in their hearts and minds.

The church should be where Jesus is truly honored and esteemed. When Jesus is truly honored, there should be healings and miracles in the lives of His people. When we don't see that, we must ask whether or not the church has become like the hometown of Jesus. Could it be that one of the reasons we don't see more healing and the miraculous in God's house isn't just a lack of faith but a lack of honor? With service after service things can become more and more common to the point that Christ is no longer truly honored.

For example, when those from a congregation are asked to pray for others. What is your attitude toward them? Do we treat those praying for us with appropriate honor? To honor them would mean that we have a real appreciation and the fullest expectation of their ability to get hold of God for the prayer need? How often do members of a congregation limit what they could possibly receive from their leaders or fellow believers by diminishing in their minds their ability or gifting?

How would things change in relationships and community if we were quicker to honor each other and gave more compliments and gifts of thankful appreciation to others?

Many believers are trying to have faith and believe God for many things. But are they respecting and honoring those in authority over them and their fellow believers? There seems to be a pervasive and general cynicism in today's culture toward authority of any kind, and it can spill over into the church.

John the apostle stated a powerful spiritual principle: "If anyone says, 'I love God,' yet hates his brother, he is a liar. For anyone who does not love his brother, whom he has seen, cannot love God, whom he has not seen" (1 John 4:20). Do you see the direct correlation between loving God and loving man? In order to love God, you must love your brother or fellow man.

We need to see that this principle applies to honor too. It could just as easily read that in order to honor God you must honor those representing Him. You can't be dishonorable of leaders, brothers, or anyone else in the congregation and think you have real honor for Jesus. Remember Nazareth's loss.

HONOR INSIGHT

While we recognize the need of honor for authority it is important to note that we should never allow anyone to lead us into evil or disobedience to God's Word. This is not about allowing dictators to command obedience contrary to the Word of God.

The apostle Peter made this clear when he said, *"We must obey God rather than men!"* (Acts 5:29, NIV). When God's will is clear and without debate and someone tries to force you to ignore God and obey them instead, you are obligated to give first allegiance and obedience to God.

However, the choice of obedience should not be used as an excuse for anyone to disregard legitimate authority or fail to give honor to God's appointed leadership. It is important to remember, *submission does not really begin until you disagree with someone.* Walking around while in agreement isn't submission; it is accord, harmony, or approval. You aren't really submissive until you walk with someone you disagree with. Submitted would also mean not murmuring or complaining while you are walking and serving with them.

Sometimes believers elevate themselves or their own opinions. It's possible to look at a leader that God has placed over you and think that the leader isn't as smart as you or know as much as you. It may well be that he isn't as intelligent or schooled as you or others in the group, but if he is chosen by God to lead and has the anointing and gifting of leadership, then he is to lead, and you are not. This is a typical pattern for God. Scripture says:

But God chose the foolish things of the world to shame the wise; God chose the weak things of the world to shame the strong. He chose the lowly things of this world and the despised things—and the things that are not—to nullify the things that are, so that no one may boast before him. (1 Corinthians 1:27–29)

The issue of honor is all throughout the Scriptures. In the New Testament Paul says, "Children, obey your parents in the Lord, for this is right. "Honor your father and mother"—which is the first commandment with a promise— "that it may go well with you and that you may enjoy long life on the earth" (Eph. 6:1–3, quoting Deut. 5:16, NIV). Paul is giving instructions to children on how to live and act in a godly manner toward their parents. The significant point is that obeying the command to honor their parents has a promise, the only commandment with a promise attached, of long life on the earth.

Could it be that longer lives are directly connected to how freely we honor and respect those God expects us to honor? God said in Malachi, "Then those who feared the LORD talked with each other, and the LORD listened and heard. A scroll of remembrance was written in his presence concerning those who feared the LORD and *honored his name*" (Mal. 3:16,NIV, emphasis mine).

According to Malachi God takes note of those who honor his name. God then said that because they honored his name, something was going to happen. " 'They will be mine,' says the

Lord Almighty, "they will be my treasured possession. I will spare them, just as a father has compassion and spares his son who serves him" (Mal. 3:17, NIV). God's people are to be an honoring people. "Now to the King eternal, immortal, invisible, the only God, *be honor* and glory for ever and ever. Amen" (1 Tim. 1:17, NIV, emphasis mine).

"AUTHORITY" DEFINED

Honor is tied closely to the word *authority*, which means the power to determine, the right to control and also to command. The church needs to both honor authority over it, and exercise its own authority in this world. We need to have a basic reorientation in our outlook and our attitude toward authority and why it is significant and absolutely essential to victory.

There are large groups of people that have been taught about faith and are trying to operate in faith. However, faith won't work the way it is supposed to as long as believers refuse to honor those in authority. Believers must learn that walking in faith means acting and speaking according to the authority given you as a disciple, but it also means honoring God and the authority He has put over you.

You can declare your faith, but until you submit yourself to authority and believe God has the ability to deal with or handle those leaders over you, then you are still failing to have faith. We need to understand and define faith as *trust*. Faith is not just trusting God sometimes, but it is trusting God faithfully and continually in every area of life, including authority and leadership over us.

Understanding this concept is essential to the success of the kingdom and being blessed of God. God is simply not going to bless unbelief. The reason He won't bless unbelief is that, first of all, it is insulting and dishonoring to Him for us to not trust Him. Second, He won't give us what we can't handle. God won't be able to trust you if you're behaving like a rebel out for your own agenda. You don't give loaded guns to infants. You can't behave like an immature child and expect God to turn authority over to you.

As believers turn and begin honoring authority, they will begin to walk in faith and power. Not only will they have faith in God to work through them, but they will begin to be able to exercise authority in this world over disease, demons, and sin. They can speak to the enemy and command him to leave or move, change situations, and even move mountains of dead religion. But don't expect anything to honor your authority and obey you if you won't honor and obey God's authority over you.

God doesn't enforce hypocrisy or recognize a double standard, and the devil doesn't have to either. The old adage that says in order to lead, you must be willing to be led is true. Therefore, if you plan on acting with authority in spiritual matters then you better be willing to honor and submit to authority yourself.

Believers are God's representatives and need to walk in His authority in this world. It is His desire to release power, healing, love, and much more through His body, and it starts with honor working in faith. The kingdom advances as Christians learn to use the keys God gives them and to exercise godly authority over evil and the devil's devices. For this to happen believers must be fountains of honor and have appreciation for the authority God has placed in their lives.

THE AGREEMENT KEY

At the beginning of this chapter we spoke of binding and loosing in conjunction with having the keys of the kingdom. Matthew also speaks of binding and loosing in the context of agreement:

> I tell you the truth, whatever you bind on earth will be bound in heaven, and whatever you loose on earth will be loosed in heaven. Again, I tell you that if two of you on earth *agree* about anything you ask for, it will be done for you by my Father in heaven." (Matt. 18:18–19, emphasis mine)

It seems obvious that another key to the victory of the kingdom is the authority found in agreement. It's very important to see that the agreement spoken of in this text is not describing a couple of people simply deciding they will say they agree about any old thing in order to get something from God. You have to read this text in the larger context of Matthew. He was talking about the kind of agreement witnesses in a courtroom have when testifying to what they have seen or experienced.

Scripture declares that everything should be affirmed out of the mouths of two or three witnesses (2 Cor. 13:1). The idea of having two or three witnesses is used several places in Scripture for various situations but always with the idea of the two agreeing on the truth. In Israel's judicial system it took two or three witnesses to convict the accused and therefore enable the system of justice to work (Deut. 17:6). Take note that the system of justice was able to function with witnesses but was limited or hindered with a lack of witnesses.

It's no wonder the devil works to keep God's people divided and in disagreement, and it is also no wonder the longest recorded prayer of Jesus was for His followers and their unity (John 17). In this prayer, Jesus is not praying about having every believer agree on every jot and tittle of the doctrines of Scripture. He is praying about the unity of churches believing together as one about His accomplished work and spiritual power so much so that His purposes are accomplished in them and in this world.

Matthew continues with this revelation: "For where two or three come together in my name, there am I with them" (Matt. 18:20). Jesus was not talking of two or three people who just happened be standing around chatting and talking about the same thing. He is talking of witnesses to the power of God, the forgiveness of God, the resurrection of Christ, the outpouring of His Spirit, and the in breaking kingdom of God. Believers with this agreement of experience and faith are the center of God's Presence on the earth. This kind of agreement in testimony and confession will move mountains of failed dead religion. As believers agree in their testimony to the work of Jesus a powerful happening is released and this key to the kingdom opens the way. This happening is an infusion of faithfulness to God and the release of real and true worship of God.

CHAPTER 7

REAL WORSHIP

The keys of the kingdom, powerful as they may be, are forged in the light of true worship. Jesus said: "Yet a time is coming and has now come when the *true worshipers* will worship the Father in spirit and truth, for they are the *kind of worshipers the Father seeks*" (John 4:23, emphasis mine). It is clear from this statement that God the Father wants and is actively *looking for* worshipers. However the text makes it clear that it isn't just worshipers God is seeking but *true worshipers*.

Today, there is a lot of talk among different groups of Christians about the subject of worship. Christian churches look for worship leaders. The Christian music industry invests in song writers and works to develop worship music. There is ongoing debate among churches and leaders about the "appropriate" form of worship service. Worship leaders, musicians and singers are increasingly important to churches that incorporate music in their worship. They are especially important to those

churches that put a strong emphasis on what is called contemporary praise and worship.

There are all kinds of issues in contemporary as well as
traditional worship services. What songs or hymns should be
used? Should there be instruments, and if so what type? What
do the people like? What do the musicians like? And a myriad
other questions. These questions lead to discussions that are
a good thing and are evidence that God is stirring hearts for
truth. The one thing we must do however, is ask ourselves
the right questions. As good as all the interest in worship and
music is—and we encourage more—it is still possible to have
many discussions about Christian worship and fail to ask the
right question.

THE RIGHT QUESTION

The right question is not what *we* like or think about our worship
that really matters. The better question is what does *God* like or
want from our worship. I think most would agree that we, as His
followers, don't always have the same priority as God. Isaiah
gave God's position: " 'For my thoughts are not your thoughts,
neither are your ways my ways,' declares the LORD. 'As the
heavens are higher than the earth, so are my ways higher than
your ways and my thoughts than your thoughts' " (Is. 55:8–9).

What is important to some believers today may not be so
important to God. Some churchgoers may think they had an

awesome time of worship, but they should ask whether God was as pleased with this time of worship as they were. What was so pleasing to them? Maybe we should ask ourselves, what it is that God is looking for in worship. What would God call good, successful, or true worship? *It is His worship, and for Him, after all.* Worship is supposed to be something where we put God first in our hearts and minds.

When you look at dictionary definitions for worship, you will find that the word *worship* is derived from the old English idea of "worth-ship." This implies the ascribing or giving of worth or value to something. If we worship Him, then we value Him so as to give our lives, time, work, honor, love, adoration, reverence, praise, thanksgiving, obedience, and, yes, even our money and all we are to God because He is worth it to us! I think a more concise definition would say that worship is simply giving everything we are to Him. This obviously should include singing and music, which is a powerful and beautiful way of expressing our worship, but it goes way beyond music.

WORSHIP DEMONSTRATED

If we look in the Bible for how worship is demonstrated and what is required, we'll gain a better understanding. The first recorded demonstration of worship occurs when the sons of Adam, Cain and Able, brought offerings to God (Gen. 4:3–4). God accepted Abel's offering but rejected Cain's offering. It's important that we see from this that not all worship is acceptable to God. There are reasons that Cain's offering or worship was rejected. However, the key element for us to recognize is that the heart of worship is in giving, and giving what God wants. *All biblical worship involves the giving of something God wants and is the essence of true worship.*

The second illustration of worship in the Bible involves Abraham and his son Isaac. God said, "Take your son, your only son, whom you love— Isaac—and go to the region of Moriah. *Sacrifice* him there as a burnt *offering* on one of the mountains I will tell you about." (Gen. 22:2). Looking past what is a horrific idea to us, to what is being asked, let us note the words *sacrifice* and *offering*. These are worship words. This is to be a costly act of worship. Notice Abraham's words as they approached the mountain: "He said to his servants, 'Stay here with the donkey while I and the boy go over there. *We will worship* and then we will come back to you" (Gen. 22:5, emphasis mine).

There is a lot of debate and controversy over this event. This story has even been used to accuse God of being a child abuser, which is totally untrue. We don't have the space to discuss all the details, but suffice it to say that God is a good and loving father. Reading this account beyond a superficial level will reveal that this story was an example for us to see what true worship is to be like. It is important to know that this event was to be a test not only of Abraham but also of Abraham's son.

Some clarity comes when we see this happening as a type of sacrifice that points to God the Father offering His son Jesus on the cross. Also, many scholars say Isaac at this time was not a baby or doubtfully even a little boy. Remember he carried a significant amount of wood up the mountain for his father as they left the donkey at the foot of the mountain. There is in fact the distinct possibility that he was as old as thirty years of age, which would make him more of a type of Christ, who offered Himself. If this was actually the case, then their submission to God's request was a supreme act of faith and worship on not only the father's part but the son's as well. It was the perfect picture of what Jesus would do. *Jesus' sacrifice was the pinnacle expression of worship and victory in a war for worship.*

THE COST OF WORSHIP

Jesus demonstrated for us the willingness to pay whatever cost necessary in order to worship God. In the Bible what was given in worship was called a sacrifice or offering, as we saw. Many of the offerings were animals people sacrificed to God. Other offerings, such as grain or money, were given as well. The standard or principle established in Scripture is clear, however. In order to worship God acceptably, all that was given was to be *the first or the best* of what the worshiper had to give. "You must present as the LORD's portion the best and holiest part of everything given to you" (Num. 18:29).

Jesus, of course, was the consummate expression of this principle as He gave Himself on our behalf. But this basic principle was demonstrated by others too. David demonstrated costly worship when he repented for taking an unsanctioned census. David was looking for the means to worship God, and Araunah, a local farmer, offered to give him the things needed. "But the king replied to Araunah, 'No, I insist on paying you for it. I will not sacrifice to the LORD my God burnt offerings that cost me nothing.' So David bought the threshing floor and the oxen and paid fifty shekels of silver for them" (2 Sam. 24:24). David's worship had to cost him something to be valid.

Later, in the gospel of Matthew, Jesus gives another example of worship: "The kingdom of heaven [God] is like treasure hidden in a field. When a man found it, he hid it again, and then *in his joy went and sold all he had and bought that field*" (Matt. 13:44, emphasis mine). Jesus wasn't talking about salvation and going to heaven. You can't buy heaven. Jesus was describing the attitude of being shrewd and sacrificially worshipping by giving the best you have as a means to experience and express the value of life in the kingdom.

The bottom line is that it costs something to worship. The cost has been paid for us in Christ. As we offer our worship, it should be given through the Spirit of God in faith that honors Christ's sacrifice for us. When David bought the threshing floor, Araunah offered to give David all that was needed, the ox,

REAL WORSHIP   101

the wood and even the altar, to worship God with a sacrifice. Technically, David could have fulfilled the law of worship, but it would not have been from his heart and spirit because it wouldn't have cost him anything and wouldn't have expressed the true value God deserved.

The cheap and easy way, the way that costs less, is always tempting. How easy it is to let our worship leaders, the band, the singers, or even other congregation members worship while we enjoy the benefits with no cost to us. David resisted that temptation and determined to pay a price. What should we do? Our depth of worship is directly related to our value of God and the cost paid. God doesn't come cheaply; you pay the full price to gain the full benefit. The heart check is to realize it really isn't how much *do I have to do* but how much *can I do*.

GOD ENABLES

True worship is possible because God has made it possible. The work of Christ at the cross extended to us the eternal invitation to worship God and do so acceptably with His provision. The *provision* for our worship is freely given to us, *but* our response is to give the *highest value* we can give. Our relationship with God through Christ is the basis of our worship. The heart of worship happens when the Holy Spirit bears witness with our spirit. The human response is love and adoration expressed fully and faithfully to God almighty.

The apostle John gave us a vision of God's invitation to worship and man's response: "Then a voice came from the throne, saying: '*Praise our God, all you his servants, you who fear him, both small and great!*' " (Rev. 19:5, emphasis mine). This was not a command but consent to continue worshipping. And the response was a magnification of volume and power: "Then I heard what sounded like a great multitude, like the roar of rushing waters and like loud peals of thunder, shouting: Hallelujah! For our Lord God Almighty reigns" (Rev. 19:6).

ACCEPTABLE WORSHIP

True worshippers will, of course, want their worship to be acceptable to the Lord. The Bible makes it clear that not all worship is acceptable. The first clear example of this is in Genesis when Cain and Able brought offerings (worship): "But Abel brought fat portions from some of the firstborn of his flock. *The LORD looked with favor on Abel and his offering*, but on Cain and his offering *he did not look with favor*. So Cain was very angry, and his face was downcast" (Gen. 4:4–5, emphasis mine). Later the writer of Hebrews declares, "Therefore, since we are receiving a kingdom that cannot be shaken, let us *be thankful*, and so *worship God acceptably* with *reverence and awe*" (Heb. 12:28).

Not only can worship be not acceptable, it can be in vain. Speaking to the hypocrite Pharisees Jesus quoted the prophet

Isaiah, saying, " 'These people honor me with their lips, but their hearts are far from me. *They worship me in vain*; their teachings are but rules taught by men.' " (Matt. 15:8–9, emphasis mine). They were going through the motions as taught but lacked a true heart of worship.

The psalmist expresses worship loudly and clearly:

Shout for joy to the LORD, all the earth. Worship the LORD with gladness; come before him with joyful songs. Know that the LORD is God. It is he who made us, and we are his; we are his people, the sheep of his pasture. Enter his gates with thanksgiving and his courts with praise; give thanks to him and praise his name. For the LORD is good and his love endures forever; his faithfulness continues through all generations." (Psalm 100:1–5)

However, we need to see that the psalmist isn't giving us an outline and form for worship. These words are a heartfelt expression, crying out as an example of true worship. The core of it all is the heart and its response to God.

Just as biblical agape love is not merely an emotion or feeling but godly actions of choice, acceptable and true worship chooses to respond to God in truth and spirit (John 4:23). If God is seeking worship, then we have a calling, and it is to worship God. Paul describes the *choice of the believer* to God:

Let the peace of Christ *rule* in your hearts, since as members
of one body you were called to peace. And *be thankful. Let*
the word of Christ dwell in you richly as you teach and
admonish one another with all wisdom, and as you sing
psalms, hymns, and *spiritual songs with gratitude in your
hearts to God.*" (Colossians 3:15–16, emphasis mine)

The worship of God is a choice made in our hearts and
demonstrated by our actions and attitudes. Feelings are not the
primary motivation to worship, God is. We choose to respond
to Him and can enjoy the feelings that come as we give Him
what He deserves.

WAR FROM THE BEGINNING

Most people would accept that worship would be appropriate
for *a true god* whether they acknowledge God or not. Then the
question might be asked: Why is worship such an issue today?
The answer is that from the beginning of creation worship has
always been at the heart of the issue of man's relationship to
God. In the garden of Eden the issue was whether Adam would
worship God or a false god. Adam, questioning the truthfulness
of God, was not just rebellious, he failed to worship. Worship
is at the crux of everything that happens in the kingdom. It is
the center of our warfare. Christian warfare is ultimately about

who is going to be worshipped by the creation, and this is the war of worship that is raging today.

Something really remarkable is the fact that man, and only man, has the capacity to worship God as He deserves. Though creation and angels may worship God, it is only man, who was created in the image of God and can give God the worship He seeks. Man, created in the image of god was the pinnacle of all creation and as such was created to be worship to God. We must realize that the question of worship is not one of will you worship, but who will you worship? The truth is, all men worship something, but not all men worship the true and living God.

This war of worship is pointed out vividly by John in the Revelation as he writes about the worship of unrepentant mankind: "The rest of mankind that were not killed by these plagues still did not repent of the work of their hands; they *did not stop worshiping* demons, and idols of gold, silver, bronze, stone and wood—idols that cannot see or hear or walk" (Rev. 9:20, emphasis mine). At another point in the Revelation, John makes it clear that all of mankind worships. The issue is simply who or what they worship. John wrote that "*All inhabitants of the earth will worship* the beast—all whose names have not been written in the book of life belonging to the Lamb that was slain from the creation of the world" (Rev. 13:8, emphasis mine). John is not talking about some sudden compelling undeniable and unique urge to worship a beast. The revelation is simple.

All of mankind worships, and to worship any God other than the true God is to worship a beast.

The worship contest is revealed for us by Satan in Matthew's gospel: "Again, the devil took him to a very high mountain and showed him all the kingdoms of the world and their splendor. 'All this I will give you,' he said, 'if you will bow down and *worship me*.' Jesus said to him, 'Away from me, Satan! For it is written: "*Worship the Lord* your God, and *serve him only*" ' " (Matt. 4:8–10, emphasis mine). Don't make the mistake of thinking this was only an attempt to defeat Jesus. Though that was true, the root of what was happening here was that the devil was seeking worship. Realize that this worship would not have been just a mere bending of the knee or prostrating himself on the ground, but the devil meant the total and fullest extent of worship: the giving of value, esteem, and deference.

The idea of the devil trying to get Jesus to worship at his feet demonstrates the incredible boldness and audacity of Satan. As unthinkable as it is, it points out the truth that the devil is not primarily trying to take souls to hell, he is actually looking for worshippers and to be worshipped. The prophet Isaiah made a statement that is usually attributed to the devil and reveals his root motives:

You said in your heart, "I will ascend to heaven; I will *raise my throne above the stars of God*; I will *sit enthroned on the mount of assembly*, on the utmost *heights of the sacred mountain*. I will ascend above the tops of the clouds; *I will make myself like the Most High.*" (Isaiah 14:13–14, emphasis mine)

The significance of worship is alluded to in another verse from the book of Revelation. John records the words of Jesus declaring His return and the giving of rewards: "Behold, I am coming soon! My reward is with me, and I will give to everyone according to what he has done" (Rev. 22:12). Jesus proclaimed that He was coming and would reward those for what they had done. So a valid question that should be raised and asked is do the words "what he has done" refer to worship? Obviously, God is looking at our worship and it fits with the context of this book of Scripture. The implication is that our worship would determine how we will be rewarded.

THE WORSHIP ENVIRONMENT

Let's look at another illustration of not just worship, but the worship in heaven. What is *God's environment* like? Remember Jesus taught us to pray, "your kingdom come, your will be done on earth as it is in heaven" (Matt. 6:10). Jesus was sharing with us revelation of both God's desire and His intentions. This revelation is more than just hopeful language; it was instruction about how to pray in faith, expecting it to happen. It would seem that Jesus was telling us to pray for heaven on earth, or at least as much as possible today. Without a doubt God's will involves more than just our obedient compliance to His commands. Heaven is the abode or environment of God, and He wants to expand His environment.

Let's look in the book of Revelation at part of John's vision of the worship in heaven and take note of what he saw there. John wrote:

Each of the four living creatures had six wings and was covered with eyes all around, even under his wings. *Day and night they never stop saying*: "Holy, holy, holy is the Lord God Almighty, who was, and is, and is to come."[9] Whenever the living creatures *give glory, honor and thanks* to him who sits on the throne and who lives for ever and ever,[10] the twenty-four *elders fall down before him* who sits on the throne, and *worship him* who lives for ever and ever. *They lay their crowns before the throne* and say:[11] "*You are worthy*, our Lord and God, *to receive glory and honor and power*, for you created all things, and by your will they were created and have their being." (Revelation 4:8–11, emphasis mine)

If we look beyond creatures and elders, we see an environment that's surrounding the throne of God.

Heaven is filled with declarations of God's holiness, glory, and honor. Expressions of thankfulness are constant and fill His ears continually. There are repeated expressions of His worth and greatness. This is a true worship environment before the true God. Our value and honor of God is to be reflected in all aspects of our life as we give Him what He deserves. This is actually what we were created for and without doubt surpasses the idea of simply singing in church, listening to a sermon, or reciting words. The issue is that if people have difficulty expressing praise and thanksgiving in church, then what is their worship life really like? More than this, are we creating an environment that pleases God.

A worshipful environment is an environment that answers the prayer of Jesus, "on earth as it is in heaven" and enables the fullest purpose of God to be fulfilled. A major truth that is not always recognized about worship is that it is an exchange. God can never be bought, though there is a cost to our worship. When we give Him the worth, value and esteem He deserves, it opens our hearts to His presence and what He brings.

Worship and the exchange that God desires for us only happens one way. Lukewarm hearts with careless and indifferent attitudes fail in the exchange as they create impotent,

vain, and fruitless worship. This is not attractive to the Spirit
of God. When true worshippers recognize the value or worth of
God and offer themselves from an open loving heart, they will
be transformed. Hearts filled with understanding and appreciation of the worth of the God we are worshipping will intensify
the relationship we now have with Him. As He responds to
our worship, the exchange of life and prosperity in Christ only
increases, and we are changed. We win and He overcomes
through us.

CHAPTER 8

THE POWER OF FAITH

As a people of faith we have to ask ourselves, how do we function as a corporate body of believers? The apostle Paul calls Abraham "the spiritual father of those of faith" (Rom. 4:11). He made his home in the promised land by faith (Heb. 11:9). Faith establishes our behavior and the kingdom of God in our lives. The bible says, "for everyone born of God overcomes the world. This is the victory that has overcome the world, even *our faith*." (1Jn 5:4, NIV emphasis mine)

FAITH DEFINED

So, the pertinent question is, what is faith? Often when trying to define faith teachers will turn to the book of Hebrews and quote "Faith is the confidence that what we hope for will actually happen; it gives us assurance about things we cannot see." (Heb. 11:1, NLT) However, this isn't a definition of faith, this is a description of faith working in us. Also, often quoted is "And without faith it is impossible to please God, because anyone who comes to him must believe that he exists and that he rewards those who earnestly seek him." (Heb. 11:6, NIV) This verse points out the essential necessity of faith but isn't a definition either.

To define faith we need to once again look at the beginning of man's relationship with God in Genesis. The beginning of the end of man's ability to please God was when Adam and Eve listened and agreed with the devil's question, "Did God really say" (Gen. 3:1, NIV) and doubted, not God's existence, but His truthfulness, faithfulness and goodness. Man implicitly called God a liar and deceiver. This was a total perversion of man's purpose in creation, that of honoring God and His Word by faithfully trusting in Him as the truth, the way and the life. For man to believe or have faith in anyone more than God was a horrific insult and the end of man's ability to know the truth and represent the Lord.

Ever since, on the earth there has been a war to know the truth. This contest is about who you will have faith in, who will you trust faithfully without doubt, to be the true and loving God of life. The simple definition of faith is trust in God and His Word as the truth and to trust it continually, faithfully and fully. Faith is actually the action of continually trusting God, that's it.

THE MEASURE OF FAITH

For someone to act in faith there has to be an object or person that they are trusting in. Faith has to have an object for there to be trust action. God's Word gives us the object of faith to place our trust in when Jesus says, "Do not let your hearts be troubled. Trust in God; trust also in me." (Jn 14:1, NIV) Jesus is to be the object of our faith and the basis of faith.

Another scripture about faith says, "Do not think of yourself more highly than you ought, but rather think of yourself with sober judgment, in accordance with the *measure of faith* God has given you." (Rom. 12:3, NIV emphasis mine)

When some believers talk about faith it is often in terms of how much or how little. When they read the above verse they see it as proof that everyone has a different amount of faith and then fall into the trap of measuring themselves to determine how much faith they have. The question is always, do I have enough faith and how can I get more? Because of our tendency to think of the word measure as meaning an amount, I believe we miss the real truth of Paul's word to the Romans.

Since Paul said to think in accordance with the measure of faith God gave them, we have to dig into his meaning of measure. The word measure used here in Greek is "*metron*". It can mean a measured portion or it can also mean an *instrument for measuring* like a measuring stick or instrument.

So, maybe another understanding of this verse is that God

gave us a standard or example for measuring faith. Could it be that Paul was not saying that God gave us a certain quantity or strength of faith, but Paul was instead saying that Jesus demonstrated and established a faith standard or measuring stick of faith for believers to use or consider. In this case, Jesus is our measure. He is the standard and supreme example of faith for all men.

Jesus accomplished what He did, not because He was God but because, as a man, He faithfully trusted His Father. He then became the one who we should look to, not only as the standard of faith but also as the source of faith for us to trust in and receive from. You see, it isn't actually about how much faith we have but it's about His faith and how much He won for us. Think about it. Don't look at what you have or don't have, but look and consider who you know and what He did and now does for you and in you.

Paul described the role of church leaders to the Ephesian church. He said they were "to prepare God's people for works of service, so that the body of Christ may be built up until we all reach unity in the faith and in the knowledge of the Son of God and become mature, attaining to the *whole measure* of the fullness of Christ." (Eph. 4:12-13, NIV emphasis mine) Paul was challenging us to grow into the standard of Christ.

The words of Paul to the Roman church were never intended to stir debate or questions about whether a believer has "enough faith" for anything. The apostle certainly wasn't saying there are differing "amounts" of "faith" to be compared between believers. He was saying we all have the same *standard of faith* to live by and the same example to challenge us to follow. He called them to listen, obey and have faith that they could do anything Jesus had done and even more than He did. This would happen as they trusted Jesus

The question is never whether you have *enough faith* for something. The question is will you act with faith in Jesus, no matter what? Don't think of Romans 12:3 as describing how much faith a believer might have within themselves, but the faith Jesus demonstrated and enables them to have in Him. Would Jesus heal someone or set them free then speak healing and deliverance to them for Him. Would Jesus walk in love and forgive someone that offended Him, then forgive as He would. Would Jesus prophecy, serve, help others? Whatever Jesus would do then trust in Him and do the same according to His faith.

FAITH'S GOAL

The book of Hebrews declares, "But my righteous one will *live by faith*. And if he shrinks back, I will *not be pleased with him*." But we are not of those who shrink back and are destroyed, but of those who believe and are saved." (Heb. 10:38–39, NIV emphasis mine) Other verses say, *"We live by faith*, not by sight." And "So we make it *our goal* to please him, whether we are at home in the body or away from it." (2 Cor. 5:7&9, NIV emphasis mine) What is the goal of faith?

It is very easy to talk about faith and never really consider its goal or purpose. This should be very crucial for believers because you can't reach a goal if you don't know what it is. The above verses give us the answer to my question. The texts point to the goal with the instruction to "live by faith". So, the clear and obvious reality is that the goal of faith is life, which pleases God.

Paul said "we live by faith, not by sight" because seeing doesn't enable life, only faith opens the door of real life. It is life that provides us experiences and opportunities to be as God desires. Typical worldly thinking says, "seeing is believing" but that isn't the way of Kingdom life. Seeing actually stops faith from being faith. God's life and power are manifest, not by sight or seeing ahead, but by trust and hope in Him and His Word. (Heb. 11:1)

Another verse about faith says, "So then faith comes by hearing, and hearing by the word of God." (Romans 10:17, NKJV) What usually follows from most preachers and teachers using this verse, is an exhortation to increase your faith by reading or hearing more of the word of God. It's always a good idea to study the Word of God, that's certainly true. But you don't have a faith tank that needs filling so you can be more powerful? Jesus said it only takes a little mustard seed size faith to move mountains (Matt. 17:20) and uproot Mulberry trees. (Luke 17:2)

We need to see that when Paul wrote these words he wasn't talking about a means of increasing your level of faith. What Paul was talking about was the initiation or start of faith in the life of a believer. When Paul says, faith comes, he means starts or begins and happens when the truth is heard. He wasn't suggesting a multiplication process for increasing the strength of faith in your tank. There is however an increase of life, a greater life in Christ as the believer learns of God's Kingdom and the Word of God strengthens the foundation that faith for life can stand on. As the believer gets to know Jesus and listens to His voice by walking in Him and experiencing His works then trusting Jesus becomes our way or standard of life.

The awesome truth is that man was originally created to live and never die. After all, a dead man would never do as the image of a living God. Today most people if asked, would say they like the idea of living and want to live a long life. There is even a built-in survival response and fight to live mechanism still in us that God placed in man originally. It shouldn't be hard for us to accept that it was God's original intention that man live forever. This is part of the force behind why Jesus came and made a way for man to have eternal life and be restored to His eternal status!

One thing that should stand out as you read these faith texts is that faith is not an option when it comes to living. The God kind of life is absolutely impossible without faith. When I say this, I'm not just talking about a life after death scenario, I'm talking about real life here and now. The apostle Paul wrote about this when he said, "I have been crucified with Christ and I no longer live, but Christ lives in me. The life I live in the body, I live by faith in the Son of God..." (Galatians 2:20) Though they don't know it, humanity outside of Christ, is the real walking dead. But with faith, dead humanity can be made alive by the Spirit of God and resurrected to a new life in Christ, right now. This is the goal of faith.

FAITH LIFE

I have no idea what Adam and Eve looked like nor what Eden looked like, and I don't even want to venture a guess. But Paul said that "we live by faith, not by sight" (2Cor. 5:7) so I don't have to see what they looked like or what our resurrection bodies will look like to trust Jesus. Our call today is to continually trust Jesus, the Word of God, and to live a life that reflects trust in the God who keeps His Word. Believers should celebrate life, walk in the supernatural, share God's prosperity with others and enjoy the fullness of life. (1Tim. 6:17) Faith says, without seeing what's coming, "God is preparing something that is better than we could ever ask or imagine". (Eph. 3:20)

Let's summarize with this thought. Hebrews chapter eleven, often called the bible Hall of Fame of Faith, lists men and women who made the choice to live in faith, many doing mighty works for God while not yet receiving what was promised and only seeing dimly from a distance. The bible commends them for their faith and lives. In fact it says, "The world was not worthy of them. They wandered in deserts and mountains, and in caves and holes in the ground. These were all commended for their faith, yet none of them received what had been promised. God had planned something better for us so that only together with us would be made perfect." Heb. 11:38-40 NIV) Faith in the Christ, the one they were ultimately looking to see, is a choice for life in the power and goodness of the living God. The action that pleases God is when a person decides to have faith in Jesus and live and celebrate life forever like Him! You won't always know the path before you or what might happen with time, but "faith" in Christ always gives life, no matter what. The Hebrews knew God wanted them to have life and their warriors knew how to dance, worship and celebrate life. They have a word for it, *L'chiam* which means "to life"!

FAITH OVERCOMES

Continually trusting Jesus and who He is and what He does is how we have life. What do you believe is stronger in you, your old nature or the Spirit of God in you making you new? How powerful is the new creation? God has created us to succeed and bring glory and honor to his name by overcoming the world as new creations. How Christianity is perceived in the world is irrelevant to Kingdom reality. There is in our world an attempt to diminish or minimize the reality and power of believers as God's church. The devil's plan is to keep his opposition convinced they will fail or can't even compete.

So what kind of faith do you have in yourself as a child of God with the indwelling Spirit of God? How much power and authority do you believe you have or that you should have? Jesus said, "I will build My church, and the gates of Hades (the powers of the infernal region) will not overpower it [or be strong to its detriment or hold out against it]." (Matt. 16:18, AMP). Did you hear what he said? The church overcomes.

Notice the alternate translation of the Lord's words saying that the powers of the enemy will *not hold out against it.* This translation sees the church in the aggressor role. Far too often the church has seen itself playing a defensive role in life controlled by a mentality that sees itself as just desperately holding on. But God expects His church to be on the offensive. God is saying stand up, get hold of faith, be my church and march forward overcoming the enemy. We do it by walking in Christ's love in faith until the purposes of God are accomplished and the enemy is defeated.

Being the underdog is how some Christians see themselves

today. They look out at the world and see all the conflicts, economic problems, ecological issues, humanism, secularism and just plain enmity against Christians. It is understandable how they can be intimidated by what they see and might think the church is losing the battle. Instead, we would be better to look at it this way: the bigger the enemy, the more glory God gets when He defeats those enemies. We should delight in God when He trusts us with a big job and a big call because it is all for the glory of the King.

God might make the job big and overwhelming just for your sake, and, by the way, the war is so big you can't do it in your own strength; you're going to have to do it supernaturally, by the Spirit of Christ. You are going to have to live your life obeying and living under the anointing of God. Also, it takes more than you and God alone; it is going to take a whole group of you, a community body working as one. For when He said, "Greater is He that is in you than he that is in the world" (1 John 4:4, KJV), He meant all of you together. Greater is He in you all together, than he that is in the world.

We must remember that God is bigger. Let me give you a word from the Lord: "His divine power has *given us everything* we need for life and godliness through our knowledge of him who called us by his own glory and goodness" (2 Pet. 1:3, NIV, emphasis mine). Here God says He has given us everything we need. Do we need to define *everything*? Peter goes on to tell us that Jesus calls us by his own glory and goodness: "Through these (glory and goodness) he has given us his very great and precious promises, *so that through them you may participate in the divine nature and escape the corruption in the world caused by evil desires*" (2 Pet. 1:4, NIV, emphasis mine).

We may participate in the divine nature, His divine nature, and escape the corruption that is in the world and is caused by evil desires. We don't have to yield to evil desires, but instead we can yield to His nature in us as believers. That means you can be like Jesus as you are walking around on the earth right now. You are not Him. You're not God. But if His Spirit is in you, then you are a child of God, made in His image and in His power, and you are supposed to do the things He did. You have His keys, are alive by faith and advancing as His community, the worshipping and conquering church of Jesus.

CHAPTER 9

EIGHT STEPS TO THE PROMISED LAND

The following chapters give us God's steps for accomplishing the victory and destiny He has for His church. Taken from the book of Numbers we find specific strategy for moving the kingdom forward and advancing the glory of God in this earth.

The book of Numbers is actually like a slide show of images, establishing the way of God for Israel to advance into their promised destiny. Most Christians have heard the story of how Israel was delivered from Egypt but then wandered in the wilderness for forty years before they were able to enter the promised land God had given them. Numbers records eight essential steps that allowed Israel to finally go forward into its destiny after stalling and waiting for years.

There are principles in Numbers that we need to be aware of, especially when we start talking about the church accomplishing what God wants to achieve through His kingdom people in this world today. The Bible states that the things happening to Israel were written down as examples and warnings for us, who are in the fulfillment of the ages (1 Cor. 10:11). In the day of Numbers, Israel had been released and brought out of Egypt by God, so they could worship Him (Exod. 8:1). Then He gave them His Covenant Law and called them to go forward into the promised land. The land lay before them but it was up to them to conquer and possess that land (Exod. 33:1, 34:27).

As we stated before, Israel's coming out of bondage in Egypt can easily be seen as a type or image of the lost person being redeemed from sin and being brought into the kingdom of God. However, their going into the promised land can't be a type of the believer going to heaven because we're not called to conquer anything in heaven. Actually, Israel entering the promised land is a type of the Christian believer today who enters into a promised land kind of life as they grow in Christ and are part of the advancing kingdom of God.

This life will not be free of battles or struggle if it follows the type of Israel entering its' promised land, but it will be one of power, presence, knowledge of God, and spiritual warfare. For the church to grow up and enter the promised life God has given to us for today, there are preparations to be made and steps to be followed, very much like those Israel had to make. The book of Numbers is the story of Israel's preparation and entry into the promised land, and as such it is also a pattern or example of steps and principles for the church to follow now. So let's look at the steps God gave Israel to follow and then see what He would have the church do, so we can advance into the promised land life of today.

With the beginning of the book of Numbers, Israel has come out of Egypt and traveled to Mount Sinai. It has been a little over a year, and they are now in the second month of their second year free of Egypt. While camped at Mt. Sinai, God makes a covenant with them and gives them the law through Moses, and now they are getting prepared to march into the promised land. Scholars do not know for sure how many Israelites actually comprised the nation at that time, but there was evidently a significant number. Estimates of Israel's numbers range from thousands to hundreds of thousands or even more.

One significant reality is that you can't move large masses of people through a wilderness and keep them together without making preparations. As we study Numbers, we can see the necessary actions God commanded Moses to take in order to move the Israelite multitude through hundreds of miles of rough, hostile desert terrain. There were without doubt many preparations made but there are *eight* essential major steps Moses had to take in order to get Israel, as a whole nation, into the promised land of God.

We're going to look at eight specific actions initiated by

Moses in response to God's commands. If these things happened as examples for us then it certainly follows that we should learn from them. Each step tends to build on the previous step and all were essential if Israel was to fully advance into the promised land and dwell there in God's presence where God intended them to live. It's very important that we recognize that though Moses took actions in a physical sense in his day that we are looking for a spiritual application for the church in our day. This is not about a legalistic approach to God. This is a prophetic and spiritual picture that the church needs to learn from in order to advance into God's fullest promises. As we deal with each step we will make a spiritual application from the natural actions of Numbers for today. Following is an overview of Israel's physical actions.

STEPS TO FULFILLMENT

Step one was to order a census of the people and appoint necessary leadership. By doing this they were more fully aware of how many they had with them and who they were. Leadership helped to organize and facilitate organization, movement and cooperation amongst the people.

Step two was to establish the tribe of Levi as the family of the priesthood. Their mission was to care for and transport the essential items for maintaining the tent of God and honor His presence in the camp of Israel. They actually were a family of helpers, or a helps ministry as well as a priesthood. Along with establishing this tribe as the priesthood they were then able to organize and place the tribes in positions to march and dwell together.

Step three was to deal with issues of impurity or uncleanness in the camp of Israel. God required certain standards be kept that would allow Him to dwell with them and move forward with them. Clean and unclean were defined for the people so nothing would hinder the presence of God.

Step four was to teach the priesthood how to not only bless the people of God but also how to enable the people to be a blessing for the nations. God was clear in how this was to be taught and practiced by the people.

Step five established the dwelling place of God and how it was to be supported and maintained. The Tabernacle would be the place of worship and meeting with God. Israel came out of Egypt for the purpose of worshipping God and this was the heart of the ability to fulfill this purpose.

Step six was to establish the light in the tabernacle for the ministry of the priesthood to function in worship. The candlestick, or Menorah, was the instrument of light and had to be maintained regularly to facilitate worship and ministry.

Step seven was a call to celebrate the Passover. Israel was to celebrate with a feast their release from slavery in Egypt, and remember their deliverance by the hand of God. It was established as a means of training their children and themselves to never forget, but to remember and live in the freedom God had brought.

Finally, *step eight* was to make two silver trumpets to sound the call of God. These were unique instruments to be used to call the assembly of the congregation of Israel or to signal time to advance and move the camp of Israel.

I don't believe it's coincidental that the number eight is considered the number of new beginnings by many Bible students. These steps of preparation and their resulting actions must be applied to the church today. We can learn from Israel's situation and following their lead prepare ourselves in order for the whole church to inherit and enter into the promises God has for the church in the earth today.

CHAPTER 10

STEP #1 - MEMBERS & ANOINTED LEADERSHIP

The LORD spoke to Moses in the tent of meeting in the Desert of Sinai on the first day of the second month of the second year after the Israelites came out of Egypt. He said: "Take a census of the whole Israelite community by their clans and families, listing every man by name, one by one. You and Aaron are to number by their divisions all the men in Israel twenty years old or more who are able to serve in the army. One man from each tribe, each the head of his family, is to help you. (Numbers 1:1–4, NIV)

The *first essential step* Moses had to take to get the people into the promised land, according to Numbers 1:1–4, was to establish who was in the body and appoint adequate leadership. God spoke to Moses, as the leader of the nation, and commanded him do three things. *First*, establish who and how many were in the various tribes of Israel, or take a census. The *second* thing was appoint assistant leaders to form a team to help lead and facilitate the plan of God. The *third* reason for the census was to achieve a register of those men who were able to serve in the army of Israel. All three of these actions work together to enable knowing and leading God's people in advancing into the promised land.

GOD'S LEADERS

The clear and simple truth is that people, even God's people, need adequate leaders and the first thing in God's priority list of what was needed to move His people was leadership. Notice that it started with a single leader and that God was present with him. It is amazing how many believe that it now takes an executive board or a congregational vote to assure adequate leadership in God's church. It would seem that today many doubt the Holy Spirit's ability to work through a single man, or even a team, to give us genuine leaders of spiritual humility and stature that are able to stand up and rightly lead a congregations. This isn't true and the critical point is that the church needs more than just leaders, it needs God anointed leaders who know how to enter into the very presence of God, hear His voice, follow His will, and administer in His power.

As Israel looked to move forward leadership started with

Moses, a single anointed leader. Then God added Israel's elders to help with the weight of daily judgments. *God formed a team* of elder leaders with Moses as chief leader and elder. This wasn't the end of it though. In Numbers chapter eleven it says, God took some of the spirit on Moses and put it on the seventy elders to enable them to help carry the burden of leadership. (Num. 11:16-17) It wasn't just natural ability that would suffice to lead God's people, it took an anointing. Why would we think it would be any different today?

The scripture clearly says leadership is a gift and an anointing from God. "We have different gifts, according to the grace given us . . . if it is to lead, do it diligently" (Rom. 12:6, 8, NIV). We may not know who God is appointing for today's leaders but we do know they need to be Spiritually anointed and appointed by God. They must be God's leader and not just a leader or someone who wants to be a leader.

There is however, a generally unstated belief and fear amongst people, even those in the church, that power or authority corrupts men, even Spirit-filled men, if we give it to them. This creates a problem when it comes to establishing leadership in the church. People have a fear of the abuse of authority and the corruption of leadership, so congregations fall back on the world's way to safeguard against this happening. In response to this fear, the church tries to insulate itself against human failure and corruption by having committees, boards, or congregational meetings in which the majority dictates the direction of the church. Some try to make church government a democracy.

The problem with this is that throughout history democracy or a majority vote have never been a guarantee of right action; it was a group voice that called for the crucifixion of Christ. A group can be just as deceived and wrong as an individual and giving everyone a vote in a matter can lend itself to inflated individual self-worth and prideful rebellion. Many think it is harder to fool a group than it is to fool an individual. Whether this is the case or not is actually irrelevant. The church is supposed to operate in the realm of the Spirit of God, and biblical Israel and the church were to be led as the Spirit spoke to the leaders.

Too often pastors and leaders are considered hirelings (Jn. 10:12-13), they work for the church and the official board or congregation is their boss. True elders or fivefold ministers (apostles, prophets, evangelists, pastors, and teachers) are then seen as *mere men* (1 Cor. 3:3) in the eyes of the church, and not as spiritually empowered and anointed gifts of God given to train, equip and lead the people (Eph. 4:11).

Pastors should be seen as part of a spiritually anointed elder team able to manifest apostles, prophets, evangelists, and other pastors and teachers. Biblical elders were not an official board they were *the anointed leaders* of the congregation. In fact most were fathers or parents in the community and had the heart of a parent as the key to their authority. Then, because of the anointing of God which produces the fivefold gifts, they were seen as leaders in the fivefold ministry. Any elder could be used by the Spirit to function in any capacity the Lord needed as they worked cooperatively with each other and with God.

Apostles, prophets, evangelists, pastors, and teachers were the elder team of the church. These terms were not offices of rank or authority but descriptions of the function and anointing on them as elders or leaders. The church today needs a radical reformation in both its perception of the fivefold ministry, and its willingness to support and finance not just a single leader but a leadership team.

THE POWER FALLACY

For God's people to advance into the promised land they could not be paralyzed by fear. It was fear that kept them in the wilderness wandering for forty years before they had faith to follow Joshua into the promised land. The same issue applies today. The fear that many church people have concerning authority and its' abuse is a hindrance to moving forward with God. Supporting this fear is an idea that springs from some form of this *quote "Power tends to corrupt, absolute power corrupts absolutely."* This idea has spread, even though most don't know the source.

In 1887, an English Lord by the name of John Emerich Edward Dalberg-Acton made the statement that "*Power tends to corrupt, absolute power corrupts absolutely. Great men are almost always bad men."* The first part of this statement seems to have been widely accepted as true and seems to underlie the fear and general suspicion of authority and concentrations of power, particularly in the hands of individuals, even in the church. Regardless of who Lord Acton was it does *not* mean that his words are to be taken as though they are unquestionably true, as though they were from God.

Certainly, we can understand the human concern over absolute power in the hands of one individual. Throughout history there have been horrible examples of different leaders abusing their power. Regardless of human history we need to first ask ourselves if Acton's statement is actually true? Consider the whole statement and ask yourself if you believe that "great men are almost always bad men." Jesus was the greatest of men and His disciples were great men. Are they then to be considered bad men? I think not.

Next, ask yourself if it is really power that corrupts men, or is it corrupt men that misuse power? Is there even such a thing as "absolute power" or a power that has no limit or restrictions of any kind? While the power of men may be great and seemingly unbounded, it is nevertheless ultimately limited and finite. No man is God nor does any man exercise unlimited power. Someone or something will always be there to eventually limit any man's power on this earth. If nothing else, death will certainly declare every man's limit. Why would anyone believe

Lord Acton's statement as unquestionably true? For biblical Christians an even greater question would be, is it biblical or biblically based?

People have seen or experienced weak men or women, in a fallen sinful state, abuse or misuse their power. Mankind succumbs to temptation but that doesn't mean we throw away the whole world because it is filled with temptations that some can't resist. To say that power corrupts men is like saying money corrupts men. While both money and power can lure and tempt men, neither money nor power in and of itself is evil or corrupts. The Bible says the "*love* of money is the root of all kinds of evil" (1 Tim. 6:10) not money itself. Surely the same could be said of power? The *love* of power can and does become a problem, but that does not make power or authority in and of itself evil. If it did, then the Lord would have been guilty of putting something evil on His followers for Jesus said, "I am going to send you what my Father has promised; but stay in the city until you have been clothed with *power* from on high" (Luke 24:49, NIV, emphasis mine).

There should be no doubt in the mind of a believer that mankind has been corrupted. A corrupted mankind is a mankind operating below the standard for which it was originally created. But, was it a lusting for power that corrupted mankind or was it distrusting and not believing the God who created mankind and called them to believe and obey?

To answer that question ask yourself this question, "How much power and authority did Adam have?" Adam was given dominion over the earth. He was a picture of authority and dominion. He named the animals after all, but was that his downfall? The kings of Israel all had power, but some were good and others evil. Power wasn't the difference between them, nor was it what corrupted them. The downfall of Adam into corruption began with a lack of faith in God and then making himself the authority over God's authority.

We need to know and accept the fact that the Bible never once says that power corrupts men. It is sin, not power, that corrupts man, and corrupt men, of course, will misuse power. It's true that all through history certain men and women in leadership have abused their authority and even today it is obvious there are abuses of power and privilege. But we must not minimize or cast aside the fact that it is God who sanctifies a man for leadership so he isn't beguiled by power but is able to lead in godly anointing, humility, and uncompromised integrity of character. The wisdom of God then partners a leader with fellow elders or leaders, a team to offer counsel, support, and input in decision making and ministry work. Leaders must nevertheless be allowed to lead as God directs them.

Paul made it clear that godly leadership was the gift of God. He wasn't concerned that evil was greater than the power of God to work in His divinely ordained gifts for the good of the body of Christ. In fact the letter to Ephesus was very clear and full of powerful hope and promise to the church. Paul wrote:

> It was he who gave some to be apostles, some to be prophets, some to be evangelists, and some to be pastors and teachers, to prepare God's people for works of service, so that *the body of Christ may be built up* until we *all reach unity in the faith and in the knowledge of the Son of God and become mature, attaining to the whole measure of the fullness of Christ.* Then we will no longer be infants, tossed back and forth by the waves, and blown here and there by every wind of teaching and by the cunning and craftiness of men in their deceitful scheming. Instead, speaking the truth in love, *we will in all things grow up into him who is the Head, that is, Christ.* From him the whole body, joined and held together by every supporting ligament, grows and builds itself up in love, as each part does its work. (Ephesians 4:11–16, emphasis mine)

These words are anointed and faith filled, full of vision and expectation for the church.

God wants to lead his church through his chosen people, and the body must learn to have enough faith in both God and his leaders to allow him to do that. This is the godly order and the way that God blesses, empowers and advances the kingdom.

God's church must be established around God and focused on His pleasure and purposes not the immediate needs, desires, preferences, or fears of humanity. God's leaders need to know God and obey him. Leadership in God's family is not a place for earthly, worldly wisdom to have a say. The church cannot be so oriented around the likes and desires of people that the desire of God gets less than a hearing, and there is a total failure to actually honor God in spiritual worship and obedience. If this happens then the church becomes little more than a human agency trying to build itself up on its own self-improvement programs of human betterment.

GOD'S HEAD COUNT

God not only gave Moses clear instructions to establish leaders He also required a census of the people. The census was to determine who was with them and who was qualified to serve in the army of Israel. They were not only to count but to look for the qualified. They were to find all the men in Israel twenty years and older who were able to bear arms and were physically able to serve in the army. Not everyone in Israel was qualified or able to serve in the army.

To apply this same command today would be to find out who are the members or those committed in the church. Elders and shepherds need to know who is really with them and will be faithful as a committed member of the congregation. Not only who are ready and willing, but are able to work and serve in God's house. The church needs leaders who are not afraid to set standards of commitment and support, which members are then expected to follow. Leaders must know who they can depend on to help seek the kingdom and fight the war for the promised land. This is more than just a casual and polite volunteer fellowship group; the church is something you enlist in and give your life to in order to fulfill God's purpose.

Counting heads was not an unusual act in the Bible. Remember, in the book of Acts they numbered how many were with Peter in the upper room to pray (Acts 1:15), how many were added to the church on the day of Pentecost (Acts 2:41), and they knew when they were all together (Acts 5:12–13). When Paul wrote to Timothy, he instructed the church to maintain qualifications for those to be considered for the "widow's list" (1 Tim. 5:9–10). We should remember that church membership is a privilege, and it shouldn't be taken for granted. This doesn't mean less committed people can't attend a church, but membership is like a census and will help identify who is truly part of the congregation and willing to make sacrifices to do the work of the ministry. This isn't about who is saved for heaven, but it is about who can be used and is available, willing to be trained and willing to help.

Membership classes, like Moses' census, help do this. Churches shouldn't be too anxious to call people official members. Here are some differences between church members and church attenders. Members join and become part of a body while attenders will remain as separate independent individuals. Members live to fully give what they're able while attenders live to receive for their benefit. Members come to satisfy, please, and honor God while attenders come to satisfy themselves. Members come to serve others while attenders come to be served. You want faithful members and as much as possible; you need to know who is willing to make a covenant of membership from their heart to be a loyal, faithful, and edifying member of the body.

Leaders must seek to know who in their congregations are truly committed to Christ and also if these same believers are committed to them as leaders in building the kingdom of God. Not everyone in a church is necessarily fully committed to the leaders. Elders must find those who are with them and who they can count on to be loyal and to actually fight to advance the Kingdom with them. Elders should put their energy and life into that kind of person and make disciples of them, and they in turn will make disciples of others.

A DIVISION OF LABOR

The last part of the command in Numbers was to choose "one man from each tribe, each of them the head of his family, is to help you" (Num. 1:4). Israel was to have tribal leaders or heads to help with the administration and work of God's plan.

Those people, being leaders in their own tribe, would know the people and their character already. The census was to help find leadership and administrative gifting among the people. Chief leaders or senior pastors will always need associates who have a relational heart and can help keep connection with the larger congregation while carrying the governing authority and power of God. Churches should have a chief elder or pastor and assisting elders or associates able to help lead and serve.

Boards made up of laymen, people who just know business and trades, do not meet the standards required of biblical leadership, and nowhere in the Bible will you find a board of deacons running the church and hiring a pastor. The religious system of today has generally failed to establish a true team of pastors or fivefold ministering elders who are able to lead in the church. The first thing Moses did was number the people and find out who was able to be in the army. Then he put leaders from each tribe or group in place. This had to happen before Israel could go anywhere toward the promised land, and it's the same with the church of today.

Then, along with having the right leadership and form of leadership in place, it is also essential to know who is actually walking with and supporting the leaders. The prophet Amos revealed the truth when he wrote, "Do two *walk together* unless they have agreed to do so?" (Amos 3:3, emphasis mine). The point of this verse is not to emphasize agreement but walking together. It is impossible to get to an agreed upon destination without walking together in the same direction with the same goal in mind. This verse highlights the need for agreement in order for elders and leaders to know who the soldiers are.

It is God's plan for churches to not only have good leaders but to also develop leadership training or discipleship for those with obvious leadership gifting. Senior leaders need to recognize their helpers and then help the congregation to recognize the gifts in the body—and that these gifts are from God and should be honored and helped to develop.

It is also true that there are sometimes would-be leaders trying to fill the calling of leadership, but they lack the capacity to adequately serve as a leader. For the good of the church and the welfare of these individuals they need to find their true strengths and be placed in positions where they can succeed. There are always those people who want to be or think they should be in front but have not been chosen or gifted by God to do so.

Even men gifted as pastors have, in some cases, not necessarily been called or gifted to serve in the chief elder role. Those men may need to step back and truthfully evaluate their gifting. They may then need to submit themselves to true senior pastors or elders with effective and visionary leadership anointing. By aligning or working under that kind of leader they will then be in a better position to help accomplish the purposes of God.

This will put things in proper order, enabling them the freedom to be what God actually gifted them to be and facilitate the preparation for moving into the promises of God. The church has struggled for far too long because it refuses to honestly evaluate and speak helpfully to each other in truth and love about what actual abilities and anointing people have.

Additionally, the church is no place for those who simply want a platform from which to preach or a place to thrust themselves forward for personal gain and glory. The church is not just about preaching; it's also about worshipping, equipping, building, and serving. The church was never about personal advancement and position.

The Word of God instructs us to take the lower seat until asked to come up to a higher place. It is time for those who just like to preach and be acknowledged to see their weakness and repent, get in position under real leaders, and let the Lord build his church. True gifts and abilities will make themselves evident and then recognition will be freely given by those in authority to those humbly serving and building the kingdom of God rather than the kingdom of man. There was a division of labor as well as leadership in Israel and so the church.

CHAPTER 11

STEP #2 - ORGANIZED HELP TO ADVANCE

The total number was 603,550. The families of the tribe of Levi, however, were not counted along with the others. The LORD had said to Moses: "You must not count the tribe of Levi or include them in the census of the other Israelites. Instead, appoint the Levites to be in charge of the tabernacle of the Testimony—over all its furnishings and everything belonging to it. They are to carry the tabernacle and all its furnishings; they are to take care of it and encamp around it. Whenever the tabernacle is to move, the Levites are to take it down, and whenever the tabernacle is to be set up, the Levites shall do it. Anyone else who goes near it shall be put to death. The Israelites are to set up their tents by divisions, each man in his own camp under his own standard. The Levites, however, are to set up their tents around the tabernacle of the Testimony so that wrath will not fall on the Israelite community. The Levites are to be responsible for the care of the tabernacle of the Testimony." (Numbers 1:46–53, NIV)

The *second essential step* required to advance God's people was to *recognize and assign helpers*. Moses needed help, not only in organizing and moving the immense number of Israelites through the wilderness, but also in moving the tabernacle of God. There are debates among scholars about the exact number of Israelites. Regardless the exact number, it was still an incredible job for Israel's leadership. If you take the number of men twenty years old or more who were able to serve in Israel's army . . . the total number was 603,550 (Num. 1:45–46). Multiply that by four (for one wife and two children per family as a conservative estimate) and you come up with 2,414,200, and that doesn't count the tribe of Levi. Moses is conservatively getting ready to move 2.5 plus million people from Sinai to the promised land, which was hundreds of miles away. I challenge you to lead a dozen people through one of the currently popular shopping malls in America without losing one or two of them. This had to be supernatural. And though it was supernatural, there had to be order and organization. There were certain things that had to be done even though God's presence was all around them.

THE MINISTRY OF "HELPS"

Moses took a census of the people, set leaders in place, and then set the people in order and *gave them jobs and positions to maintain.* They began to assign tribes, camps, and divisional groups to certain positions they were to maintain in both the march and in camping. This was not a mob. This was an orderly procession marching and moving together. They had banners held up over each group or tribe to help locate them and keep them together. They were given a position in which they were to march and a position where they were to camp around the Tent of Meeting. Today, this would be like finding out people's gifting and abilities in the church and assigning them the best tasks to help advance the Kingdom. Good soldiers aren't called to gripe about their position; they're to just do the best job they can.

What pastors need is a church made up of people who are adaptable and pliable, able to be placed in positions like chess pieces. Chess pieces do not fuss or complain when you move them around. Christians are too often quick to complain and say, "that's not my calling. I don't have time for that or isn't there something else I could do?" Believers must realize their opinion and estimation of themselves is not what matters.

When people are asked to rate or evaluate themselves, they can easily miscalculate. (2 Cor. 10:12) Individuals making estimates of their own talents and ability often have opinions that are far from reality. For the church to succeed we need

God's valid estimate and not ours. Moses had to move a huge number, maybe as many as 2.5 million people, hundreds of miles through a hostile dessert. No wonder Moses wanted to quit. Most of us would want to quit too. But I doubt Moses asked anyone "where do you feel called to serve?" It sounds more like they were placed in position and expected to keep their position and to fulfill their responsibilities.

In addition to placing the many tribes into divisions and ranks, Moses was also told to separate out the tribe of Levi. He was not to number them in his census or include them in the army. They were given the task of caring for and moving the tabernacle and all its furnishings. This was a perfect example of what the Bible calls a "helps" ministry (1 Cor. 12:28). The Levites, also considered the priests, maintained the mobile house of God for the nation of Israel. They camped around the tabernacle when the nation camped and acted as a buffer zone to safeguard the people from accidentally wandering into holy ground and accidentally dishonoring or defiling the holy place and possibly dying because of it.

FIRST HELPS PRINCIPLE

There are two basic principles revealed in the setting apart of the Levites. First, the church needs people to *honor the helps ministry* in the church. The Bible says, "Each of you should look not only to your own interests, but also to the interests of others. Your attitude should be the same as that of Christ Jesus: Who, being in very nature God, did not consider equality with God something to be grasped, but made himself nothing, taking the very nature of a servant, being made in human likeness." (Philippians 2:4–7)

Jesus set the example of *true ministry, which is to serve* God and His people. The call to serving isn't to humanity in general but to the covenant people of God, the body of Christ, and anyone who would follow Christ. The body of Christ must recognize the divine importance of serving and being a help. It should be natural for the servant hearted to give honor and appreciation to those that serve, but it is important that the whole church give honor to serving.

The tribe of Levi took care of God's tabernacle for the people of God. This is a picture of the helps ministry in the church. Far too many people come to church expecting to be served rather than taking their place as servants. The simple truth is that Israel could not have traveled and entered the land of promise if the Levites hadn't faithfully served them, and God, as called and assigned. Believers must have the same humble servant hearts if the church is to conquer the enemy. It is absolutely essential that believers today step up and shoulder the ministry of helping God's appointed leaders get things prepared and ready to serve the people at every opportunity. Every job in the church is important and needs to be done efficiently and willingly if the body is going to enter into the promises of God.

THE SECOND HELPS PRINCIPLE

The second basic principle is that *God chooses and equips different people with differing amounts of responsibility and ability*. Not everyone gets to do the same thing, nor should they expect to. God may not be a respecter of persons when it comes to judging sin (1 Pet. 1:17, Col. 3:25, Rom. 2:11–12), but he does pick certain people to do certain jobs.

God said he had selected Paul for a particular mission (Acts 9:15), and when Jesus went up on the mount of transfiguration, he didn't take all the disciples with him; he took only Peter, James, and John, leaving the others behind. Even when Jesus taught the parables, he used the illustration of differing amounts of talents or money being given to different servants and the testing of their responsibility with what they had been given. The point being that there isn't an equality of distribution of God's gifts or abilities between all his people. Though, we need to remember that everything is subject to possible change and growth.

Most people have the natural ability to speak a language but not everyone is a gifted teacher or preacher. Many like to sing in the shower or fancy themselves as musically talented, but the truth is that only some are actually gifted, talented enough to perform in Carnegie Hall or actually lead God's people in praise and worship. Most people can pick things up, rearrange furniture, or throw out the trash but not all are good at organizing or designing a better arrangement of things in the most attractive or functional way.

Lots of people might like to be doctors, scientists, or physicists but as much as they may want to be this not everyone has the intellect, talent, or drive to achieve every dream they might have. Some can run a mile in under four minutes or high jump over seven feet while others, because of limitations, can only wish. Everyone can do something but not all can do the same things equally as well as the other. This is especially true when it comes to supernatural "gifting" or anointing by God. The thing to remember is that God is always looking to transform and change the way things are and that includes giftings and opportunity. We just need to be faithful.

The church needs to accept these two principles and allow the leadership over them to make the assignments as necessary for the accomplishing of the purposes of the church. Moses established an order and arranged the people of Israel, so they could more effectually function and move smoothly as an immense unit. Likewise, the Bible calls the church to meet and function smoothly as a unit when it says we should encourage each other, "not forsaking the assembling of ourselves together, as is the manner of some, but exhorting one another, and so much the more as you see the Day approaching" (Heb. 10:25, NKJV). The word *assembling* means being called out to assemble together to accomplish an objective. It isn't just coming to a meeting but being brought together and then fitted and equipped to function together for a purpose. It is the ordering and arranging of our individual gifts and talents for the purpose of accomplishing a goal.

For Moses the goal was to take 2.5 million Israelites into the promised land. For the church the goal is to be the powerful representative of God on earth, walking in his presence and power and sharing the good news of the Kingdom with as many people possible until Jesus himself returns. The last part of the verse in Hebrews says, "so much the more as you see the Day approaching." You don't have to be a great mathematician to calculate that the day of the Lord is closer now than when that verse was written. Therefore it is all the more important that we be about the business of assembling as God's church.

Assembling is a call to be gathered or connected into a corporate functioning unit. While many little "cells," or smaller gatherings, may be building blocks, the goal is for the larger corporate body to be united and strong. The ultimate goal is not small groups with many lesser leaders continually reproducing but with no real cohesive oneness and vision of largeness. The kingdom of God is not a collection of little kingdoms but one large encompassing kingdom. There were twelve tribes in Israel, but God's goal was always one nation entering the promised land. There is a place for small groups or cell groups, but the focus must always be on the corporate body, the church assembled. This is the destiny of God's people and serving and helping each other accomplish all we can is a means to that end.

EXCELLENCE NEEDED

One final aspect to the helps ministry mind-set that is absolutely essential to the kingdom war effort is that of excellence in ministry. As divine order develops in a church and people are positioned in the right place and begin to function, it is important to instill in them the value of excellence in everything they do. Paul encouraged working to have gifts but also to excel in gifts that built up the church: "So it is with you. Since you are eager for gifts of the Spirit, try to *excel* in those that build up the church" (1 Cor. 14:12, NIV, emphasis mine).

It's important that jobs are not just done, they should be done with excellence. And in order for a task to be done with excellence, one needs to be trained in the skills or the job they are to master for the kingdom. Training is essential for success and for excellence in any task needing to be done. For a simple example, if you want the lyrics of songs projected for worship, then you need someone who is not only capable but efficient, caring, and dependable. Teach them not only the technical aspects of the computer, of putting the words up and anticipating change as the song moves along but teach them excellence. They must be responsible to be at every service or make sure they have a replacement capable of doing the job every bit as well as they or even better. They should be prepared and alert to any eventuality and change. Excellence desires to do everything with the best reflection on the ministry of Jesus and His church. God is excellent and we want to be like Him.

Excellence doesn't mean perfection. It is a measurement of quality of effort! To excel is to go beyond the average or norm. It means listening to what Jesus said and going the extra mile or giving what you weren't asked to give. Look for people with this quality of character. Excellence is a sign of Jesus' imprint on their heart, and it is reflected in their character image.

An example from the life of Abraham might help to reinforce this point. When Abraham sent his servant to find a wife for Isaac, the servant didn't know what woman would be right for his master's son. The servant wisely prayed and asked God to make the woman known to him. God heard his prayer and pointed out to the servant the future wife of Isaac.

The girl, Rebekah, was shown to be the right person to fill the role of Isaac's wife by the extra effort she made towards Abraham's servant. He came to Rebekah's hometown, leading a string of camels needing to be watered. He stopped by a spring where the townswomen were coming to draw water. The servant prayed that God would bring the right woman to him. When Rebekah came with her jar, the servant asked for some water. Rebekah responded by not only giving the servant a drink of water but also offering to give his camels water as well. She went beyond what he asked; she offered the servant a drink and then said, "I'll draw water for your camels too" (Gen. 24:19). Any woman, who was willing to water ten camels was certainly worthy to be the wife of Isaac.

We can laugh, but God pays attention to character and a willing sacrificial heart. They serve his purposes with reward. The church must have excellence in its workers if it wants to defeat the enemies of the kingdom. The testing of the Lord's servants and their stewardship always comes down to excellence and its rewards. When doing something for God, the phrase "it's good enough" doesn't exist. Nothing we have is good enough for him, so we do the very best we can all the time because he is worthy of our best. Remember the foolish servants who didn't have enough oil to last the night? Always be prepared to go above and beyond, this is kingdom business and the way to victory.

CHAPTER 12

STEP #3 - STANDARDS FOR LIFE

The LORD said to Moses, "Command the Israelites to send away from the camp anyone who has an infectious skin disease or a discharge of any kind, or who is ceremonially unclean because of a dead body. Send away male and female alike; send them outside the camp so they will not defile their camp, where I dwell among them." (Numbers 5:1–3, NIV).

The *third essential step* for preparing Israel to move into the promised land was to establish God's *standard of cleanness* or health in the camp of the Lord, where God was going to dwell. This text is pointing to physical or ceremonial issues of uncleanness that would defile or contaminate the camp, making others ill and defiling the dwelling place of God. Since Israel was to be an example to the other nations, it had to reflect the cleanness and health, not just of individual bodies but also community, inherent with the presence of a Holy God. A Holy God doesn't dwell amongst common disease, sickness and sin. In the time of Moses, the physical uncleanness represented to man the need for cleansing in order to not only be acceptable to God but to represent life with God. The believer today should realize that the physical issues were actually meant to speak of the more significant need of spiritual cleansing from sin and its' effects that Jesus provides.

We should note that immediately following these verses dealing with physical issues of cleanness and disease there is a section dealing with interpersonal life and relationship problems in the community of Israel. This whole chapter was addressing the need for the people of God to be whole in every way. God wanted Israel to represent to the world what a people dwelling in the presence of the one true and holy God would look like. He wanted them to have a life that was clean, not only physically but relationally, emotionally and spiritually. A people made whole and filled with life and love for God and each other. It was to be attractive and a way of life other nations would long to experience. So God establishes standards for Israel that would enable this life.

THE CLEAN AND UNCLEAN

In the opening text Moses is called to deal with physical issues of being "clean" and "unclean" that would prevent health and the presence of God in the camp of Israel. The church should learn from this to recognize the problem of having "clean" and "unclean" hearts that affect the work of God in the assembled congregation today. James wrote, "Come near to God and he will come near to you. Wash your hands, you sinners, and purify your hearts, you double-minded" (James 4:8, NIV). James readily equates being double-minded, or having two minds, with having an impure heart. Earlier in James' letter as he discusses a double-minded man he says, "That man should not think he will receive anything from the Lord; he is a double-minded man, unstable in all he does" (James 1:7–8, NIV).

The man that cannot decide whether he believes God and stand in single-minded faith is unstable and not able to bring the things of God into his life. Probably the greatest sin man can be guilty of is to doubt the integrity and veracity of God. To question or deny the existence of God is tragic, but to admit His existence and then ignore Him or call Him a liar is evil and is an affront of devilish proportions. To be double-minded and unbelieving is to be unclean from a sinful heart of unbelief creating a place where God can neither dwell nor operate in power. This is not the life God wants for His people.

The irony of this impossible situation is that sinful

unbelieving hearts are only purified by faith. Listen to how Peter describes the work of the Spirit with the gentiles desiring to know God: "He made no distinction between us and them, for he purified their hearts by faith" (Acts 15:9, NIV). Notice that the purification of their hearts came by faith or believing God. The unbelieving or impure heart, while dishonoring to a Holy and righteous God, binds the sinner in his unbelief and keeps the presence of God at a distance, along with the cleansing or blessing He would bring.

God took great pains to make it clear that there was a difference between something common and something given over and acceptable to God. Moses was commanded to recognize and establish a distinct line between what was acceptable and unacceptable in the camp of the Lord. Israel was to be a witness, a testimony to the goodness of a faithful and holy God. Their story and life were the image of God's presence with His people. It needed to be clean and righteous.

This had nothing to do with whom God did or didn't love but what was acceptable in the camp of the Lord. The idea of a people having the presence of God among them is a serious business. God does not dwell in just any place or anyone. The people that God chose were to be distinct in all the earth, a special people set apart or holy unto the Lord. The prophet Micah spoke of the inspired future of God's people and their distinction: "And you will again see the distinction between the righteous and the wicked, between those who serve God and those who do not" (Mal. 3:18, NIV).

The church can be far too casual in its attitude toward the presence of the living God and the accompanying life of God it represents. The typical church is usually much more aware of, and careful about, the presence of visitors and themselves, than they are of the presence of God. His presence can be tangible and experienced in varying degrees but not by the casual or uninterested. Those who approach God casually not only lose the blessing of His presence, they also dishonor and disrespect God through their demeanor. God has standards and He won't stay in substandard dwellings or places where there is a lack of appropriate honor and respect. When hearts treat Him as common, or as some ordinary or insignificant thing, there will be a powerless absence of His Holy presence and fellowship.

THE GRACE ISSUE

Part of the reason there can be such a casual attitude toward the Lord in the church today is because of teaching that has promoted an inaccurate and unbiblical definition of grace. This teaching depicts grace as a totally unconditional favor and acceptance by God which is completely indifferent to our behavior. Biblical grace is certainly an unmerited favor, but it is a favor that, because of Christ, empowers and enables the transformation of heart and behavior that God desires. The body of Christ cannot display a casual and distorted view of the Lord any more than Israel could live as unclean people and still demonstrate themselves as the people of God.

The belief that there are no real requirements or expectations on the part of God promotes a kind of perpetual state of failure and indifferent casualness concerning the things of God. This spiritual condition comes from incomplete repentance, presumption of forgiveness and ignorance of God's word. These false ideas of grace actually promote the kind of sick or unclean people that do not represent the true image of God and His life.

THE IMAGE ISSUE

Church people that think they are "under grace" and therefore it's wrong to put any expectations or requirements on them are wrong. For them, the grace of God is freedom to be or do anything without any fear of consequence because they abide under the perpetual forgiveness of God. They fail to acknowledge there is more at stake than their personal forgiveness. There is a total rejection of their responsibility to be an example of the cleansing and life changing God the world needs to see.

In Genesis it is revealed that man was created in *the image of God* (Gen. 1:27) Since man was created in the image of God it was his mission to be the image of God to the rest of the creation. When Adam sinned he distorted and marred the image of God but Jesus came and restored God's image. Jesus said to Philip "Don't you know me, Philip, even after I have been among you such a long time? *Anyone who has seen me has seen the Father.* How can you say, 'Show us the Father'?" (John 14:9, emphasis mine) Now we are called to be like Jesus (Col. 3:10) and once again be the image of God.

A false grace creates a false image because the Lord is not seen as the jealous God who deserves and demands our faithful honor, obedience and worship. Too many believers are content with a powerless God—that is, until they are in a crisis, and then of course, they want a real God with the power to respond to their need.

When believers truly acknowledge Jesus as the all-powerful God, they have to allow Him to change who and what they are. He will be the Lord they bow to, honor, and serve at all times. Their love for Him will be insatiable and motivate them to levels of obedience and sacrifice they never knew were possible. This is the image standard God would have today.

God's calling Moses to set standards for the clean and unclean were to establish both the image of a godly people but health amongst those people. It was for the good of the people and their mission to represent the Lord. That has not really changed today, even though Jesus totally fulfilled all of God's righteous requirements for us.

THE IDENTITY ISSUE

Consider the situation with Ananias and Sapphira. They were members of the early church. In Acts we see Peter called them out and asked,

> Ananias, how is it that Satan has so filled your heart that you have lied to the Holy Spirit and have kept for yourself some of the money you received for the land? Didn't it belong to you before it was sold? And after it was sold, wasn't the money at your disposal? What made you think of doing such a thing? You have not lied to men but to God." When Ananias heard this, he fell down and died. And great fear seized all who heard what had happened. Then the young men came forward, wrapped up his body, and carried him out and buried him." (Acts 5:3–6, NIV)

Peter, as a leader in that congregation, challenged Ananias and charged the couple with agreeing to test the Spirit of the Lord (v. 9). Now that couple certainly didn't openly or verbally say, "Let's test the Spirit of the Lord." but it was *their behavior and what they said to the church* that was considered, by God, to be testing the Spirit. Sapphira and Ananias were unclean or double-minded in their commitment and giving to God.

God so closely associates with the body of Christ that when that couple attempted to deceive the church, it was as if they were trying to deceive and test the Holy Spirit Himself. This is the very same kind of identification that Jesus expressed to Paul at his conversion. Paul had been tormenting the church and Jesus appeared to him on the road to Damascus and asked him, "Saul, Saul, why do you persecute me?" (Acts 9:4).

Peter was a man just like any man today and was operating in the grace and Spirit of God when he challenged Ananias and Sapphira about their hearts and behavior. He was operating in love for them, for Christ, and for His church, and the result brought a wholesome fear of God to the church. It also changed the image of the church and how the people of God appeared to the world around them. It took grace and faith for Peter to call out two members of the church in his responsibility before God to the church. We need the same kind of spiritual strength in leaders today.

The reality is that as the church becomes more conformed to the image of Christ then God and the power of His presence will become increasingly more evident. With His presence there will be a purifying of hearts in church congregations and demonstrations of power similar to what happened in the time of Acts. In fact, as the body of Christ matures and becomes what God has intended, His presence will become more and more tangible to the hearts of His people, and they will in turn call out for more of His Spirit and grace, not just enough to help them get by but to help them be all they can be in Him.

The church is to know Him for who He really is and will fulfill their mission in this earth.

A NECESSARY SEPARATION

God told Moses to put certain people with particular diseases or issues He considered unclean outside the camp so they wouldn't defile the whole camp. God loves everyone, but he especially loves and values His church (His body) and will protect and work for the common good of the group. Likewise, leaders today have to love and value the individual but never above the welfare of the group or their common good. Bad attitudes can be infectious and spread, creating spiritual disease or division between members.

What must happen is not legalistic enforcement of arbitrary rules. Instead, leaders must have the true Spirit and strength of character to be godly examples of grace as they hold a line of distinction between clean and unclean in the congregation of the Lord. Some pastors and congregations may have to be willing to let some people leave their church, or in some cases even ask unrepentant and divisive people to leave. We must enact church discipline, not in a punitive sense, but as a call to rise to God's standard of life and purity of heart, for the Lord that won't be satisfied with less.

Church leaders need to be willing to confront attitudes that threaten to infect the whole congregation. People who question the actions of leaders, challenge goals, sow suspicion in other members, or just generally stir up discord and dissension among the people need to be confronted. This should not be a harsh or mean spirited thing but a necessary and caring interaction. The Bible is clear on these matters. Paul wrote, "Warn a divisive person once, and then warn him a second time. After that, have nothing to do with him" (Titus 3:10, NIV). To responsibly pastor a church means being willing to correct issues in people's lives.

Pastoral confrontation may momentarily reduce the church in size, but it will build it up in the Lord. Eventually God will reward fidelity and faithfulness. The church not only will grow, but it will be spiritually stronger and more effectual in building the kingdom.

THE MANIFEST SPIRIT

Leaders have to pray and respond with action for the things of God to happen. While we are praying, we should be working to establish a standard of excellence in congregational life and worship that establishes an acceptable dwelling place for God. Just as Moses had to strive to establish purity and holiness in the camp of Israel, we must strive to establish purity and holiness within the church because God won't come and be present with us without it, and we won't be able to move or conquer anything or anyone without Him.

Remember, this is not about a purity of perfection but a

love of God and purity of faith—a faith fueled by desire and passion, hunger, and thirst. The Bible says, "Blessed are those who hunger and thirst for righteousness, for they will be filled" (Matt. 5:6, NIV). God comes to those who in faith truly hunger and thirst for Him. Understand that faith is not just an intellectual knowing *about* God but a faithful trusting *in* God that produces a real and tangible experience *with* the Spirit of God.

It is also good to realize that the manifest presence of God should not be limited in our understanding. God manifests Himself at various times in multiple ways, as He works in us, through us, on us and around us. The Spirit of God is Omnipresent as God, He's everywhere at the same time. Yet He can come in very personal and specific ways or in public expressions of power. He can speak prophetically, touch hearts to transform, release revelation, healing, deliverance or conviction. For example when the Spirit of God was poured out on the day of Pentecost there was a limited manifestation in the upper room with the disciples that not everyone experienced. Then similar expressions happened at other times as the church grew in the book of Acts (i.e. chapters 8, 9, 10, and 19).

We have to fully grasp the need for God's presence. Without His presence we cannot go anywhere nor do anything productive for the kingdom. Moses knew the truth when he said, "If your Presence does not go with us, do not send us up from here. How will anyone know that you are pleased with me and with your people unless you go with us? What else will distinguish me and your people from all the other people on the face of the earth?" (Ex. 33:15–16, NIV). His presence is the distinguishing difference between the people of God and people who dwell in a double-minded kind of "impurity" and "unclean" doubt and unbelief without a real hunger or thirst for Him or His kingdom. Paul declared the standard of life in Christ when he said, "*those who are led by the Spirit of God are sons of God.*" (Romans 8:14)

CHAPTER 13

STEP #4 - BEING A BLESSING

The LORD said to Moses, "Tell Aaron and his sons, 'This is how you are to bless the Israelites. Say to them: " ' 'The LORD bless you and keep you; the LORD make his face shine upon you and be gracious to you; the LORD turn his face toward you and give you peace." ' " "So they will put my name on the Israelites, and I will bless them." (Numbers 6:22–27, NIV)

The *fourth essential step* in preparing Israel is described in Numbers 6. The Lord said to Moses, "Tell Aaron and his sons *this is how you are to bless the Israelites*." God gave Moses specific instructions as to how the priests of Israel were to bless the people of Israel. The words he gave Moses were not just a simple prayer asking God to be nice to Israel nor were they a formula to be routinely repeated, they were God's words revealing and releasing His desired blessing of Israel.

These were words commanded by the Lord to be spoken and invoked upon the nation of Israel, the elect people of God moving to the promised land. They were to be declared by God's elect priesthood. These words were to be spoken in faith, fully anticipating God's fulfillment of them, to assure the Israelites that the Lord himself would honor them and keep his Word to them as a people receiving His favor, provision, and protection. The last verse of the blessing indicates that this is how the Lord's name will be put upon the Israelites and that he will then bless them as the people of his name. The abiding presence of God's blessing and favor would label Israel as a people that had not only his favor but also his name on them, showing them to be his covenant people. The blessing of Israel would in turn enable and cause them to be a blessing to the entire world.

THE BLESSING

This blessing is actually an expression of the principle of sowing and reaping and is to be demonstrated by Israel. God desired His people to be blessed. To facilitate this He wanted the spiritual principle—being blessed is meant to produce the blessing of others—to be lived out before His people. God sowed His blessing into a people that would in turn bless others for the glory of God.

Having the Lord's name linked with Israel was to be a mark

of identification and favor bestowed upon them. God wanted Israel to not only be blessed, but He wanted to be identified with them as His blessed people, and then for them to be a blessing to others. This declaration was to instill an attitude of being the blessed and favored of God in His people who in turn would realize their destiny of being the means to blessing the world around them. He wanted a continual demonstration of blessing and favor to fill the hearts of Israel, so they could bless others and eventually the world would know the goodness of their Holy God.

The ultimate fulfillment of Israel being a blessing was of course the coming of Jesus through the physical line of Abraham. Today the kingdom high priest, who is still invoking a blessing, is Jesus. "Therefore, since we have a great *high priest* who has gone through the heavens, *Jesus* the Son of God, let us hold firmly to the faith we profess" (Heb. 4:14, NIV, emphasis mine). The Bible also declares, "Praise be to the God and Father of our Lord *Jesus Christ, who has blessed us* in the heavenly realms *with every spiritual blessing* in Christ" (Eph. 1:3, NIV, emphasis mine). It also reveals that "because Jesus lives forever, he has a permanent priesthood. Therefore he is able to save completely those who come to God through him, because he always lives to intercede for them" (Heb. 7:24–25, NIV). Jesus' ministry as high priest is to intercede and *invoke every spiritual blessing* of God to save completely those who come to God through him.

The power of a blessing was recognized all through the bible. It is clearly seen in God's word to Abraham. (Gen. 12) The idea behind biblical blessing is one of invoking the authority God has endowed on people like a leader or father. The child or the one following that leader receives the fulfillment of the declared pronouncement by the hand of God. For example note the drama of Jacob and Esau, each seeking their father Isaac's blessing. Regardless of the differences between them, Jacob and Esau both strongly desired and believed in the significance and power of their father's blessing and Esau wept when he could not receive the blessing. The church will only benefit from recognizing the power in this practice as we see that God instructed Moses to make sure Israel's priesthood continued to declare the blessing and release this word of God to His people. The practice continues in the ministry of Jesus and His followers empowered by the Holy Spirit and speaking the prophetic blessing on His children.

This is the intent God had for the Israelite priesthood and the blessing invoked in the book of Numbers for that day. Today God's leaders, fathers or any child of God can speak blessing over others by the Spirit. The Spirit has given words to believers that mean much to those being blessed but more important is the idea of a people living to be a blessing to others.

The priests were trained and instructed by Moses to proclaim to Israel the blessing of God's favor. They asked that He would watch over and protect them with his divine power and presence. Not only that, but that He would also look upon them to deal kindly with them and be gracious to them. God would turn toward them, be with them, and grant them his shalom (peace, contentment, and friendship). This is precisely what Jesus does for all His believers today.

Moses was commanded to ensure the priests knew of this blessing and to be sure that the nation of Israel understood that it meant God was establishing them as his nation. The priests were to pronounce God's goodness and help the people fully comprehend the abundance of God's favor towards their nation and His plan to cause them to be a blessing in the earth.

Leaders of the church today need to do the same thing. Pastors should instill in the people of God the same basic understanding about the intent of God. The body of believers, God's church is God's holy priesthood today, with Christ as the High Priest. (Heb. 3:1, 1 Peter 2:5) God wants to build His church by using His priesthood, pronouncing blessings and being a blessing to the world around it. The principle is powerful and the same today as in Israel.

LEADERS OF BLESSING

The kingdom of God needs real leaders who are able to be a blessing and teach the people to bless and live as a blessing. Pastors and teachers have taught the church much but we need a church that blesses, fathers and mothers who release blessings on their children and teach them to bless others. Believers, family and friends that are a community of blessing and help in a world looking for hope.

A crucial step in getting God's people to advance into the promised land and win their battles is to have leaders who know how to be a blessing to God's people. In the day of Moses the priests had to be taught what to say so as to invoke and establish the blessings God intended. Leaders today need to know how to lead people into the presence of God and fully realize how blessed they are.

The greatest blessing and exchange of blessing occurs during worship. Leaders must be worshippers in order to lead the congregation into worship and the presence of God. To win the battles we face and move into the promises God has given the church, leaders must learn how to present the blessings and help the people know how to live in them and become an expression of God's blessing to the world around them. It is God's intention to identify with his people to such a degree that his name is seen on them and His presence is among them on a continual basis.

In faith the church is to seek the face of the Lord, to actually gaze upon Him and to marvel at Him. Someday the Bible says we who believe will actually see His literal body and marvel at Him (2 Thess. 1:10). But today he still wants us to marvel at Him in faith and love Him zealously. Knowing their blessing will enable the body of Christ to establish thrones of true praise for Him to inhabit and have fellowship with His followers as they bless Him.

Leaders are called to lead in worship, be examples of worship, and usher their congregation into the very presence of the Lord. Too many pastors or evangelists see themselves as preachers or teachers, and they are really neither if they are not first of all worshippers. They are to establish the blessing of God through heartfelt, passionate worship of the living God. Just as Moses was to teach Aaron and the other priests how to invoke God's favor with the right words, today pastors and leaders are to establish the blessing of God in creating a worshipping, faithful, and obedient people.

Moses built a tabernacle after the heavenly model according to the command of God for the worship of Israel. Today, we should establish praise and worship as close as we can to the passion and glory of heaven in our church gatherings. We need less form and more substance in our exaltation of the Lord. Without true worship and an atmosphere that is alive with his presence and power, we will never be able to move into the promises of God. Just as Israel needed the priestly blessing of Numbers 6 when they were in the wilderness, today the church needs the empowering worship and blessing of God's presence if it is to move forward with God.

The words of Moses in the beginning of this chapter are

actually a declaration of both God's favor to Israel and a prescription for what we need in order to fulfill our destiny today. We need him to bless and keep us. We need the Lord's face to shine upon us and be gracious to us. We need the Lord to turn his face toward us and give us *shalom.* We certainly need Him to bless us with His shalom.

This isn't just some high and lofty dream but the way of God and a reality that will actually allow God's people to have His power and presence in the midst of their worship. Godly pastors who lead the way in worship and forthrightly teach the whole Word of God will cause the flourishing of his Spirit and truth. God's presence, power, provision, and protection will be the blessing upon His body. As these things happen, the Lord will put His name upon the church and give it shalom. Then He will receive honor, glory, and blessing.

CHAPTER 14

STEP #5 -
TEMPLE TITHING

When Moses finished setting up the tabernacle, he anointed it and consecrated it and all its furnishings. He also anointed and consecrated the altar and all its utensils. Then the leaders of Israel, the heads of families who were the tribal leaders in charge of those who were counted, made offerings. (Numbers 7:1–2, NIV)

The *fifth essential step* to entering the promised land given in Numbers is to *establish the dwelling place of God and receive offerings to support it*. Moses built a tabernacle or tent fashioned after the pattern of the heavenly tabernacle as the writer of Hebrews explained: "They serve at a sanctuary that is a copy and shadow of what is in heaven. This is why Moses was warned when he was about to build the tabernacle: 'See to it that you make everything according to the pattern shown you on the mountain' " (Heb. 8:5, NIV). In the time of Moses the dwelling place of the Lord was a kind of tent that later, in the time of Solomon, became a beautiful building, a wonder of the world.

But now, the Scriptures make it clear that it is not a building that God desires but a people that he calls a temple: "Don't you know that you yourselves are God's temple and that God's Spirit lives in you? If anyone destroys God's temple, God will destroy him; for God's temple is sacred, and you are that temple" (1 Cor. 3:16–17, NIV). The dwelling place of God is in His people. Of course those people need a place or building where they can assemble and give corporate worship to God, but how easy it is to forget that now it is the people that are significant and the first priority to God.

Paul addressed this forcefully when he said, "If anyone destroys God's temple, God will destroy him; for God's temple is sacred, and you are that temple" (1 Cor. 3:17). It seems very clear that God was not talking about a physical building nor was he advocating a particular way of gathering together. What seems very clear is that God treasures His people and that He wants them together for His purposes. It's only as the people are together that they can be a blessing to each other and corporately to God. The truth is that God dwells in His people and the only building He inhabits is the one created by His people wherever they gather. What we need is an adjustment in our understanding of God's intent and purpose when He first had Moses build the tabernacle for Israel.

THE TABERNACLE

Remember the Scriptures tell us that God was very specific when He instructed Moses to build the tabernacle. God's instructions fill three chapters of Exodus. He instructed the construction of not only the tent but elaborate gold and silver furnishings, spices and oils, garments for the priests, and expensive materials for the structure of the tent itself. God said, "See that you make them according to (exactly like) the pattern shown you on the mountain" (Exod. 25:40). The tabernacle was meant to be an example to Israel of God's heavenly dwelling, and it was also a type of Christ and his work of salvation for man. Christ was the highest and most precious price ever paid to build a temple. So Israel's extravagant giving was merely a picture for us that pointed to what Jesus was going to give for His temple.

The whole nation of Israel brought offerings to aid in the tabernacle's construction. They offered gold and other materials until they brought so much the leaders commanded them to stop:

> So all the skilled craftsmen who were doing all the work on the sanctuary left their work and said to Moses, "The *people are bringing more than enough for doing the work the LORD commanded to be done*." Then Moses gave an order and they

sent this word throughout the camp: "No man or woman is to make anything else as an offering for the sanctuary." *And so the people were restrained from bringing more, because what they already had was more than enough to do all the work.*" (Exodus 36:4–7, emphasis mine)

This is one of the most incredible sections of Scripture in the Bible. What an awesome picture of giving, which is actually the truest form of worship, to fulfill God's plan. This example sets the standard for how God's people are to respond to the work of God. The question, though, is what is the work? What does this picture of Israel mean for us today?

It means God is assembling ever-increasing groups of people of various sizes and equipping them to invade and conquer the promised land. He wants His people to be His representation in the earth. God is empowering His children to be loving and anointed men and women of God, enabling them to be families and servants that honor and glorify His name and kingdom. He wants His people to be a people with healing in their hands and deliverance in their mouths, a prophetic sound to dispel the enemy while building and guiding His people.

God's purpose is that we reflect His heavenly image accurately on this earth. He really doesn't care much about the building that houses His assembled people or how elaborate it might be. He always looks inside our buildings into the beating heart of life that is His presence and not at the building itself. He is looking for a people willing to give Him all their worship in order to see the work of God done on the earth—to see Jesus return to a glorious bride and the fullness of God's kingdom established on earth.

The tabernacle of God was a place of worship and for God to meet with His people, but it was something more as well. The tabernacle was built to be mobile and move with the people, or actually the people moved with it. The tabernacle housed the ark of the covenant, which represented the presence of God. Remember Moses' famous words: "Then Moses said to him, 'If *your Presence does not go with us, do not send us* up from here. How will anyone know that you are pleased with me and with your people unless you go with us? *What else will distinguish me and your people from all the other people on the face of the earth?*" (Exod. 33:15–16). The presence of God established and distinguished the people of God in the earth. It is the presence of God that matters and should be the driving force in the church today.

There are those who argue against buildings as though buildings take up too much time, attention, and resources that could be used to more directly minister to people. On the other side of the picture are churches that invest tremendous amounts of time, energy, and resources in building campaigns, striving to get people to give and fund their operation. We need to open our eyes to the reality that buildings are actually irrelevant to the real problem.

Buildings are inanimate and only tools to be used by people. If people don't have the Spirit of God or simply don't use their facilities wisely, it isn't because of the building. Nor is it a reason to stop meeting in large buildings and go to small group type meetings. In small group settings there is a decentralization of church authority and ministry and a weakening of corporate anointing and power. Small gatherings have their place, but it is not to take the place of the unified and assembled body of believers worshipping and following established and anointed leadership.

The dividing of forces into small groups can, at times, play into the hands of the enemy and allow the building of many little kingdoms with small groups of disciples following many immature would-be leaders. God's biblical pattern has always been to assemble the people together and move them together. Israel could not go into the promised land until the whole group went together with the presence of God. The real issue isn't about buildings or group size. The real issue is the failure to build the house of God, the true temple of God today.

The prophet Haggai addressed a similar issue:

Then the word of the LORD came through the prophet Haggai: "Is it a time for you yourselves to be living in your paneled houses, while this house remains a ruin?" Now this is what the LORD Almighty says: "Give careful thought to your ways. You have planted much, but have harvested little. You eat, but never have enough. You drink, but never have your fill. You put on clothes, but are not warm. You earn wages, only to put them in a purse with holes in it." This is what the LORD Almighty says: "Give careful thought to your ways. Go up into the mountains and bring down timber and build the house, so that I may take pleasure in it and be honored," says the LORD. "You expected much, but see, it turned out to be little. What you brought home, I blew away. Why?" declares the LORD Almighty. *"Because of my house, which remains a ruin, while each of you is busy with his own house.* Therefore, because of you the heavens have withheld their dew and the earth its crops." (Haggai 1:3–10, NIV, emphasis mine)

God wants His church built. He is tired of men building their own kingdoms and their own houses for their own personal glory. He even says through the prophet that the reason there is a lack of prosperity among the people is because they have been giving their time, energy, and resources to building something other than His house. The principle is as true today as it was then. They were selfish and self-centered in their lives. He advised them to think carefully about where they put their efforts. He obviously wanted their attention and a change of their ways.

The same is applicable to the church today. It isn't the dwelling place of God that has been built. There is no place or reason for competition between churches. As long as there is agreement in the essentials of the Christian faith, there should be fellowship and cooperation. Leaders must see themselves on the same team, working to honor God, even if there are some minor doctrinal differences. Members of a church don't belong to one leader or even a team of leaders, they belong to God because He purchased them. The issue is, are they growing in relationship to God and to each other. God wants to dwell in His house in such a manner that His presence is obvious in the healthy relational community of His children.

This is not to say that there is absolutely no presence of God in churches but there is far less than what ought to be in a vibrant assembly of God's people of faith. Paul, when talking to the Corinthian church, one of the most charismatically gifted churches in the New Testament, said, "That is why many among you are weak and sick, and a number of you have fallen asleep" (1 Cor. 11:30, NIV). Because the believers of this church refused to recognize themselves as the body of Christ, caring for and serving each other while giving honor and reverence to God, they were becoming weak, sick, and some were even dying. They were coming under judgment for failing to judge themselves, and God was removing His presence from among them. They in turn were reaping the fruit of God's absence, and not having His power and glory in their midst, they were becoming weak, sick, and dying.

God wants a group of people who recognizes they are set apart for His use and purpose. He wants a group that knows they are His and are equipped to do the work of the ministry, and be a blessing, not just individually but corporately.

TITHES AND OFFERINGS

Not only does God want His people to do the work of ministry, He also expects the people to support, with their time, energy and material substance, the upkeep and work of the ministry. God's leaders are to set the pace when it comes to giving and then also to collect offerings from the people. They must teach the people about the finances of God's kingdom and how His economy works. It is a divine ministry to receive tithes and offerings and build the dwelling place of God. God's ministries should operate debt-free with more than enough money and resources to do whatever needs to be done to extend the kingdom.

Leaders who actually believe and live God's Word will be faithful to the principles of living in God's kingdom and constantly display and teach tithing, giving, and prosperity. They will also explain that God wants no less commitment to sharing in every area of all the people's lives. The people must believe and commit to corporate unity and serving so that everyone is contributing their part all the time. The church must have and follow leaders that know how to bless the people. These leaders will lead the people into ministry that can operate without debt. These leaders will be a blessing to the people and then the people in turn can bless God as the ministry flourishes; there is no debt so you keep going forward. Leaders and ministers need to learn to do this for it is God's way of finance.

It's not unusual for leaders to stand up and become apologetic when they talk about taking an offering. No apology should ever be given when taking an offering unless the church is misusing what is being given. If you really believe it is a way of blessing the people and supplying the work of God, why in the world would you apologize? We should search our hearts and ask why so many people are sensitive to hearing talk about money and giving in God's church.

Today there are extreme teachings about money and prosperity. Some teachers have taken Scripture out of context and interpreted biblical blessings as some kind of get-rich-quick scheme. This is obviously far from the truth of God's Word. However, on the other side of the giving and prosperity issue are those who want to equate poverty with spirituality. They say that the fewer material goods people have, the more committed and truly spiritual they are. Another perspective is a kind of Christian socialism whose proponents advocate a total sharing of finances and possessions. Finally, a fourth group might teach minimalist living where believers are supposed to get by on the barest necessities possible and give all the rest to the poor. Sadly all these concepts miss the truth greatly. Part of the scheme of the enemy is to promote lies and confusion in an effort to prevent the growth and the prosperity of the kingdom.

First, obviously it takes money to do the work of the kingdom. Keeping God's people chasing false ideas about riches and wealth so they miss the true intent of God derails many of the children of God. However, getting people to accept poverty as God's plan, when the Word says that poverty is a curse, takes another part of the body out of the provisional blessings of God. The third and fourth groups fall into the trap of giving up what God has given to them as a blessing so they don't have anything to invest in the kingdom when there is a need. It is high time for the body of Christ to embrace biblical and sound teaching that promotes the prosperity and blessing of God's family.

God's people are not to be captured by wealth or riches, but neither are they to run from them or ignore the legitimate need for them in the kingdom. God wants to bless His children materially as well as spiritually. In fact the word "profit" is not an evil word. Jesus appeals to the desire in man to profit when He said, "For what will it *profit* a man if he gains the whole world and forfeits his soul? For the Son of man is going to come in the glory of His Father and His angels, and will then *repay* every man according to His deeds." (Matt. 16:26-27, NASB) Would Jesus appeal to an evil motive to produce righteous action? No!

While greed and avarice are sinful and not to be part of our motivation in life, profit is a God given motivation. Wasn't it a desire to profit that God used when talking about the rewards given to a productive and faithful handling of talents, or money? "Take the talent from him and give it to the one who has the ten talents. For *everyone who has will be given more*, and he will have an abundance. Whoever does not have, even what he has *will be taken from him.*" (Matthew 25:28–29, emphasis mine) Even God Himself wanted to profit and He sowed a man into the creation to reproduce and produce a harvest of God's image in the world. Sowing isn't evil, every farmer as well as business man practices it on a regular basis, and sowing is done in the anticipation of a harvest, a profit. It is foolish for Christianity to try and avoid this reality. The false ideal of giving without any desire to receive some sort of reward is not biblical nor is it Godly, and actually contrary to the righteous way God created man.

As the prosperity of God is released in the body, His children will have the capacity to give and support whatever the Lord wills. John said, "Beloved, I pray that you may prosper in all things and be in health, just as your soul prospers" (3 John 2, NKJV). Some have tried to explain away the simple truth of these words, but John understood the plan of God. His people should bring life and prosperous blessings wherever they go.

I am not going to take the space to deal with the arguments

against tithing as though it is part of the law. Suffice it to say that tithing was initiated long before the giving of the Mosaic law. Tithing was primarily a way of honoring God by giving Him the first and best part of everything they harvested. Tithing is just a starting point for the worship of God, and those that have trouble with tithing actually have more problems than just a failure to tithe. Giving is ultimately a test of true spirituality and love. Paul openly challenged the church to give and said he would test their love by their giving (2 Cor. 8:8).

All that we have is God's, but He will let us manage the 90 percent (or whatever percent we hold back). He then watches to see what we do with it. If we handle whatever we have well, then He will let us have more. But if we have problems giving him even just 10 percent, then don't expect to move into the truly blessed category of stewardship. Jesus explained stewardship well:

Take the talent from him and give it to the one who has the ten talents. For everyone who has will be given more, and he will have an abundance. Whoever does not have, even what he has will be taken from him. (Matthew 25:28–29)

God blesses those He can trust to be a blessing to His kingdom and to others.

God expects the church to live by sowing and reaping.

The church must learn to thrive financially for it is part of the function of God's kingdom and His means of financing the move of His people into the promises to come. Pastors must not shrink back from teaching and endorsing the goal of prosperity for all of God's people. It is a truth that will work anywhere in the world if given enough time, and the people are faithful to God.

The prosperity of God's children is supposed to be one of the clearest signs to the rest of the world that God is favoring and blessing his covenant people. Joseph is one of the best examples of how this is supposed to operate (Gen. 39–50). God wanted to use Israel as an example to all the world of what the one true God would do for a faithful covenant people. Israel largely failed in their covenant, but Joseph didn't. The church must not, and by the grace of God will not, fail in its covenant but will succeed to the greater glory of God.

This step toward the promised land is so important. The church must ask itself whether it has been giving itself entirely, till told to stop, to build God's house. Have you been building God's house or some other house? The call is to give without reserve to build God's temple on earth till it is a blessing. And those who are like Jesus Christ are the temple of God today. We are the place of His presence and the purpose of all that He does today.

CHAPTER 15

STEP #6 - HOLY SPIRIT LIGHT

The LORD said to Moses, "Speak to Aaron and say to him, 'When you set up the seven lamps, they are to light the area in front of the lampstand.'" Aaron did so; he set up the lamps so that they faced forward on the lampstand, just as the LORD commanded Moses. This is how the lampstand was made: It was made of hammered gold—from its base to its blossoms. The lampstand was made exactly like the pattern the LORD had shown Moses." (Numbers 8:1–4, NIV)

The *sixth essential step* of promised land preparation is to *establish and confirm the ministry of the Holy Spirit* of God. Usually, when people talk about the work of the Holy Spirit in the church, the first thing they talk about is either the fruit of the Spirit listed in Galatians chapter five, or maybe the supernatural gifts listed in First Corinthians chapter twelve. You don't have to look far to find teachings on either of these subjects. However, we want to focus our attention on the work of the Spirit that enables the priests to function and do their ministry.

LAMPSTAND SYMBOLISM

In Numbers 8, we read about seven lamps that were on a Jewish lampstand, commonly called a menorah. It stood in the Holy Place of God and enabled the priests to see and do their ministry in both the Tabernacle and then later the Temple. It's significant that the number seven is generally considered by bible students to be the number of fullness. Since the lamps were oil lamps (oil being a type of the Spirit) the symbolism ascribed to the lamps is that they represent the fullness of the ministry of the Holy Spirit. Of course lamps do one thing: provide light. The ministry we're discussing is the work of the Holy Spirit to illuminate or reveal, which allows the servant priests to accomplish their ministry.

Today the Holy Spirit illuminates the Word of God and allows it to pierce to the depths of a heart. The Spirit gives knowledge and wisdom in the way of God's Word and can help deal with situations and people more insightfully. The voice of the Spirit encourages, builds up, and comforts the children of God and illuminates our paths, or where to walk, as well as convicts us when we go astray. This is truly an essential work of the Spirit of God.

To help understand the symbolism involved notice that these lamps were oil lamps (as mentioned above) and not candles which burn themselves down and are consumed. The lamps on the lampstand burn oil that is provided from outside themselves, a picture of the believer living by the provision of the Holy Spirit living in them. The Spirit is the illuminator of truth and the revealer of God's wisdom and will and the "Counselor" (John 14:16). The people of God have been brought out of darkness into a great light (Matt. 4:16). Jesus promised the ministry of the Spirit, "But the Counselor, the Holy Spirit, whom the Father will send in my name, will teach you all things and will remind you of everything I have said to you" (John 14:26).

The lampstand was made from hammered gold from its base to its ornate blossoms using a single piece of gold. There are different speculations about the meanings of the ornamentations. Rather than speculate, let's consider the simple and plain facts given to us. First it was made out of battered or hammered gold. Gold, of course, is very precious and rare in its purest form. Refining is necessary to make gold pure and more valuable. It must be hammered or formed into a usable shape. While the light and oil of the lampstand represents the work of the Holy Spirit in the temple, or the believer, the lampstand itself, the vessel that holds the oil lamps, was made of beaten and refined gold.

Therefore, it would seem that just as Jesus, the Redeemer, was physically beaten to accomplish His work, we, the redeemed, have to be refined and hammered or disciplined, spiritually speaking, to reach our fullest beauty and most precious and useful form.

Since the lampstand was made out of a single piece of gold, it is a picture of unity and oneness. Jesus was the one way, the one redeemer, the one Lord and of course there is only one Spirit and one body. The fact that the lampstand stands on a base or foundation again alludes to Christ since Paul declares there is no other foundation or base that can be laid other than Jesus Christ (1 Cor. 3:11). The blossoms are the clearest picture of all since they are a picture of the fruitful vine. The believer is to be a vessel of the fruitful work of the Holy Spirit and a dispenser of the kind of character and life of Jesus.

The church would not be the church without the Holy Spirit, "because those who are led by the Spirit of God are sons of God. For you did not receive a spirit that makes you a slave again to fear, but you received the Spirit of sonship. And by him we cry, 'Abba, Father' " (Rom. 8:14–15). The Bible also says, "But the fruit of the Spirit is love, joy, peace, patience, kindness, goodness, faithfulness, gentleness and self-control. Against such things there is no law. Those who belong to Christ Jesus have crucified the sinful nature with its passions and desires. Since we live by the Spirit, let us keep in step with the Spirit" (Gal.

5:22–25). It is the Holy Spirit that reveals truth to us, causes us to change and demonstrate the character of Christ, to have the anointing and gifts of the Spirit to work in the supernatural realm, and to reflect the glory and image of Christ to the world around us.

THE OPERATION OF THE HOLY SPIRIT

The Bible says that it is impossible to please God without faith, so obviously faith is essential to having a relationship with God. Another important reality is that just as faith *pleases* God, the fruit of the Spirit in the believer *demonstrates* God. It is just as important to demonstrate God as it is to please Him, and it is the working of the Spirit in the believer that enables fruit and therefore a fruitful demonstration. The Spirit works in us to cause us to both *want* to do His will and to *enable* us to do His will (Phil. 2:13). The reality is that we are to have the character of Christ. We are not to just profess Christ but to be a demonstration of all that He is, especially in character and integrity.

Some people believe the Holy Spirit stopped working miracles and doing supernatural signs when the last apostle, whoever that was, died. In spite of this unbelief, the Spirit has continued down through history to confirm the Word of God and, when the environment was right, demonstrate the power of God. The Holy Spirit never stopped operating, and the church, to be the church, must teach to all its members of the power of the Holy Spirit. Peter clearly expressed the promise and blessing of the Holy Spirit: "The promise is for you and your children and for all who are far off—for all whom the Lord our God will call" (Acts 2:39)

The lamps that Moses set up represented the light, the power, and the presence of God's Spirit and His anointing in His holy place in the tabernacle. Paul declared to the Corinthians that they were now the temple (1 Cor. 3:16), meaning of course the assembled corporate body, not just individual believers. That means we are also the holy place where God wants his light and presence to reside and burn. God's Spirit wants to illuminate and drive out any darkness in us and enable our service to the Lord.

The Levites were to take care of the lamps and keep the wicks trimmed and the vessels full of oil so that the light of the Sprit would never go out or be dim. Without the light they could not minister in the Holy Place of God. This is just as true for us today as well. We are not to be like the unwise virgins who ran out of oil (Matt. 25:8). Believers need to make sure their spiritual wicks are trimmed, so they burn, and are full of the oil of the Spirit of God. We are supposed to be illuminators of God's truth and vessels of His presence. Spending time in the presence of God—praying, worshipping privately, and meditating in the Word of God in order to maintain the light of God's presence—is the responsibility of each believer. This is essential for the church to be able to operate by the Spirit of

God. It is the only way for the church to have life and not just empty, dry ritual.

THE ANOINTED PRIESTHOOD

While we are a temple for the Spirit of God in which to reside we are also called a priesthood of believers. Part of the ministry of the priests of Israel was to minister unto the Lord the worship and sacrifices He deserved. The giving of the worship sacrifices happened in what was called the outer court of the tabernacle. One of the most significant works of the Spirit is the enabling of our worship *unto* the Lord. Peter said, "you also, like living stones, are being built into a spiritual house to be a holy priesthood, offering spiritual sacrifices acceptable to God through Jesus Christ" (1 Pet. 2:5).

Beyond offering the sacrifices of worship on the brazen altar in the outer court, the next ministry of the priests happened in the holy place, the inner court of the tabernacle. It was here that the ministry of the lampstand did its work. The only light in the holy place was the light of the oil lamps of the menorah. This tells us that the light of the Holy Spirit is the only light that reveals and enables the priestly work of the holy place. Scripture says, "So he said to me, "This is the word of the LORD to Zerubbabel: 'Not by might nor by power, but by my Spirit,' says the LORD Almighty" (Zech. 4:6). God is going to accomplish victory in the warfare we face only by the power of the Holy Spirit.

The priests of God were only able to do their ministry by the light of the Holy Spirit. What the light revealed in the holy place was two ministry areas: One was a golden table holding the bread of communion and the other was a golden altar of burning incense, representing intercessory prayers to God. The work of the Holy Spirit enables us to have a continual fellowship and communion with the Lord. Jesus said, "I am the living bread that came down from heaven. If anyone eats of this bread, he will live forever. This bread is my flesh, which I will give for the life of the world" (John 6:51). When He said this He was alluding to the bread in the Holy Place. Only the priests could eat this bread and have a communion meal with Him. Now we, the redeemed priesthood, have the privilege through the work of the Holy Spirit, of consuming Him and being filled with His life.

The other place of priestly ministry was the golden altar of burning incense. The incense represented prayers of believers (Rev. 5:8). The priests were to keep the incense burning, or, in other words, they were to ensure continual prayer was going up before the Lord.

It's important that we understand that intercession is more than just prayer. The word *intercede* can be broken down into two parts: *inter* or "between" and *cede* meaning "to grant" or "convey." In other words the intercessor stands between two parties, in this case God and man, to represent one to the other and convey or grant on behalf of one to the other. Talking to God on behalf of another puts one in the position to hear from God and be able to respond to His word and help others. Jesus does this in the heavenly realm, and we are to act in the earthly realm. What we have to see is that the whole work of the priesthood is one of intercession, or one of standing before God on behalf of others. Whether it is offering the sacrifices of worship, consuming the bread of communion or offering prayers of intercession, these are all our priestly ministry. We are called to strengthen and build each other up. This is the ministry of intercession and fellowship.

STANDING IN THE GAP

The Bible uses another term for intercession, and it is a military term or concept. The idea is to "stand in the gap." The prophet Ezekiel spoke for the Lord when he said, "I looked for someone who might rebuild the wall of righteousness that guards the land. I searched for someone to *stand in the gap* in the wall so I wouldn't have to destroy the land, but I found no one" (Ez. 22:30, NLT, emphasis mine). The perfect fulfillment of this ministry is of course the saving work of Jesus. But if we are His body in this world then part of our ministry is to bridge the gap between heaven and earth and to help bring heaven's will to the earth.

The Bible gives us two examples of men who displayed the

true heart of intercession, of standing in the gap to keep the enemy out. The first is Moses. He was the leader of Israel who stood before God on behalf of God's sinful people:

> The next day Moses said to the people, "You have committed a great sin. But now I will go up to the LORD; perhaps I can make atonement for your sin." So Moses went back to the LORD and said, "Oh, what a great sin these people have committed! They have made themselves gods of gold. But now, please forgive their sin—*but if not, then blot me out of the book you have written.*" (Exodus 32:30–32, emphasis mine)

To say it another way, "If you won't forgive your people, then remove me as well from the book of life." This is intercession on the highest order.

The other example is Paul. He wrote to the church in Rome:

> I speak the truth in Christ—I am not lying, my conscience confirms it in the Holy Spirit—I have great sorrow and unceasing anguish in my heart. For *I could wish that I myself were cursed and cut off from Christ for the sake of my brothers*, those of my own race, the people of Israel." (Romans 9:1–4, emphasis mine)

Both Moses and Paul would have given their own lives to save their people if that were possible. Of course Jesus accomplished a perfect intercession, but can we settle for anything less in our own hearts?

Scripture talks about the ministry of Jesus, our High Priest, in similar terms: "Therefore he is able to save completely those who come to God through him, because he *always lives to intercede for them*" (Heb. 7:25, emphasis mine). Jesus isn't just praying for us; He is acting on our behalf before the Father. Not only is the eternal ministry of Jesus one of total intercession, but the Word of God tells us the Holy Spirit is also doing the same and helping us in our weakness and prayers: ""And the Holy Spirit helps us in our weakness. For example, we don't know what God wants us to pray for. But the Holy Spirit *prays for us* with groanings that cannot be expressed in words" (Rom. 8:26, NLT, emphasis mine)

The victories we need will never be achieved by the strength of flesh but always through the power and light of the Spirit. It isn't only strength for warfare and revelation that we need the Spirit, but He is also necessary for true worship and intercession.

God's army will win its battles by worship and prophetic intercession because intercession is more than just praying or talking to God. Holy Spirit–enabled intercession has authority. Jesus taught, " 'I tell you the truth, whatever you bind on earth will be bound in heaven, and whatever you loose on earth will be loosed in heaven. Again, I tell you that if two of you on earth agree about anything you ask for, it will be done for you by my Father in heaven' " (Matt. 18:18–19). Intercession is standing before Him, speaking and listening to Him. Then after hearing Him, speaking forth His word or His will to others in order to bridge the gap and bring forth His will on the earth. This is the ministry of the Holy Spirit as He illuminates the work of God for God's ministers. This is true intercession, and absolute essential to help and enable the move of God's people into the promised land of life.

CHAPTER 16

STEP #7 - CELEBRATE THE PASSOVER

The Lord spoke to Moses in the Desert of Sinai in the first month of the second year after they came out of Egypt. He said, "Have the Israelites *celebrate the Passover* at the appointed time. Celebrate it at the appointed time, at twilight on the fourteenth day of this month, in accordance with all its rules and regulations." So Moses told the Israelites to celebrate the Passover, and they did so in the Desert of Sinai at twilight on the fourteenth day of the first month. The Israelites did everything just as the Lord commanded Moses. (Numbers 9:1–5, NIV)

The *seventh essential step* of Numbers to equip Israel to enter the promised land was the command to *celebrate the Passover*. This wasn't the first time God had spoken to Israel

about celebrating the Passover. God had given Israel instructions about the Passover when he said, "'So this day shall be
to you *a memorial*; and you shall *keep it* as a *feast* to the Lord
throughout your generations. You shall keep it as a feast by an
everlasting ordinance" (Exod. 12:14, NKJV, emphasis mine).
It would seem obvious that it was pretty important to God that
Israel not just remember the Passover but that they regularly
take steps to faithfully *celebrate* the Passover. Actually the
significance of Passover can't be overstated.

REMEMBERING RESPONSE

God had in mind a special time when His people were to
remember vividly a past event. The Word of God tells us He
uses reminders. For example, God said, "Whenever I bring
clouds over the earth and the rainbow appears in the clouds, *I
will remember* my covenant between me and you and all living
creatures of every kind. *Never again will the waters become a
flood to destroy all life*" (Gen. 9:14–15). Certainly, God doesn't
have a bad memory or is getting old and inclined to forget things.

When God uses the word *remember*, it doesn't just mean
reflecting in the mind but being moved to actions that demonstrate the reality. It means God is moved to enforce or maintain
His promise or vow to mankind. Look at circumcision for Jewish
men. It was a daily reminder to all Israel's men that not only
had something happened to them in the past, but they were now

living in covenant with God and their daily lives were to reflect that reality. In a similar way, wedding rings remind couples that there was a day in the past when they made a marriage covenant, but today they are to act on that covenant and faithfully live out what they vowed.

So it was with Israel and the Passover celebration. They were to remember it by declaring it publicly for everyone to hear. Then they were to have a celebration, reaffirming its reality, not only as a past event but also, and more importantly, as a powerful and transforming reality demonstrated in their lives. God says to "have the Israelites *celebrate* the Passover at the appointed time" (Num. 9:2, emphasis mine). We also find God saying that it is the second year since they had left Egypt and it was time to celebrate Passover, so plan and make it happen because you need to remember not only where you came from but where you are to go.

THE NEW BEGINNING

Something very interesting happened in Egypt concerning the dating of Passover. "The LORD said to Moses and Aaron in Egypt, "This month is to be for you the first month, the first month of your year" (Ex. 12:1–2). What happened here is that God actually *changed their calendar*. It was, in fact at that time, the seventh month on their calendar, but God invoked executive privilege and declared, in effect, we're starting over this month.

Starting now, it is a new year for you.

In other words, the Passover was to be seen as a brand-new beginning in the lives of the Israelites. Thus they were to keep a remembrance of a new beginning every year thereafter and instill it, as they celebrated, in their children and their children's children. The Passover was in God's mind an everlasting ordinance and never intended to be considered just a past historical event. Passover was to be an ever-present event in their everyday lives. Man is so prone to take God's works that are a real-life changing and energizing experience and turn them into religious memories. When this happens the transforming power of that past happening loses its potentcy and ability to work in the very people memorializing the past, because they've lost the reality and its potential for the present life.

Much has been written about the various types and shadows contained within not only Passover but all the Feasts of Israel. But the most significant point about Passover is that Jesus is the chief fulfillment and reality of the feast. The apostle Paul makes a clear declaration to the New Testament believer. Paul wrote:

> Get rid of the old yeast that you may be a new batch without yeast—as you really are. For *Christ, our Passover lamb, has been sacrificed.* Therefore *let us keep* the Festival, not with the old *yeast*, the yeast of malice and wickedness, but

with bread without yeast, *the bread* of sincerity and truth."
(1 Corinthians 5:7–8, NIV, emphasis mine)

Yeast and the Lamb are both references to the Passover Feast. In appealing to the fulfillment of the Passover by Christ, Paul says get rid of your old sinful life and live a life that reflects what was accomplished by Christ and is a demonstration of what is made possible for believers now.

Paul connects the old and past with the new and now when he calls Jesus "our Passover lamb." Jesus was slain as the Sacrifice to deliver us from slavery to sin just as the Passover lambs were slain each year and used to celebrate Israel's deliverance from slavery in Egypt. The lambs were just a type and shadow that Christ would fulfill in reality. But there is also a reference in the Corinthian text to unleavened bread and Paul urges the church to live a life of sincerity and truth, a type of bread without the influence of yeast, which represents sin in mankind. The most insistent part of the text though is the command to "keep" the festival by living a life of truth and sincerity before the world. Paul's meaning is clear. The celebration of feasts or rituals mean nothing if there isn't a corresponding truth in the lives of those who have partaken of the feast. The real celebration is not supposed to be some sort of event where we just remember a past happening and are thankful, but it's actually rejoicing in Christ as we live out our lives in the Lord as an actual feast of

His goodness now.

There must surely be great significance in the wording of Numbers when the command is to "celebrate the Passover" without a reference to feast or memorial. It would seem that the emphasis here is toward making this event happen *in the lives* of the Israelites. They were getting ready, not to celebrate the *coming out of Egypt* nearly as much as the *going into the promised land*. This feast should not be so much a remembrance looking back but a prophetic celebration looking ahead at what is to come. The Lord wanted His people working to make what started in Egypt a beginning of something far greater and much more significant.

COMMUNION CELEBRATION

The application for the church today should be fairly clear. What we typically call Communion in the contemporary church is actually a remnant of the Jewish Passover celebration. When Jewish influences were pushed out of the Christian church centuries ago the connection between Passover and Communion was lost to much of the Christian world, but God certainly has not forgotten. He certainly remembers why this feast was given to believers.

So, in the same way that the Passover was never intended to be just a celebration of memories, the Communion meal today should not be just a time of looking back at the sacrifice of our

Lord. The intention of Communion was never intended to be just a time to focus on the horrors Christ suffered on our account and a quiet time of guilty introspection. The Communion meal should be a real feast. It should be a time of thanksgiving for the sacrifice of the past *and* the provision of the present as well as a celebration and anticipation in faith of what is before us. It should be a time of planning to accomplish and complete, with the power and presence of God, what is yet to be done.

The Corinthian church was weak, sick, and some were dying because they failed to recognize themselves all together as the body of Christ. Today, much of the church only see themselves as a bunch of forgiven people waiting around for Jesus to return and wrap things up. While they are waiting, they try to convince others to wait with them and "be saved."

Too much of the church today is like the church in first century Corinth. It is weak, sick, and dying of unbelief while failing to enter its' promised life. The church must wake up and celebrate the true Passover and have real communion. Christ paid the price to deliver and set His church free from poverty, captivity, blindness, and oppression (Luke 4:18).

The body of Christ is called to be the representative authority of God in this world. When the church, by the Spirit, walks with humility in faith, hope, and love before the presence of the living God, there is nothing it can't accomplish. The church was not called to wait until God does something more but to do good works and to make every effort to enter into His rest. I know it sounds strange, but *rest* here means ceasing *our* works or interests and taking up *His* works and purposes. In this way we would actually advance His kingdom of God and be His children to the fullest possible extent.

God spoke to Moses to command Israel to celebrate its Passover because he had plans for them, and He wanted them to constantly be reminded of His glory, power, and provision, which was available to them all the time. He was concerned that they would do exactly what they did: forget who brought them out of the land of Egypt. They went into unbelief and many failed to enter into the inheritance God desired them to have. How many in the church today are not going to have the reward and promised land life that God wants them to have because of unbelief and a lack of spiritual strength? Dry religious activity is deadly to an active spiritual life.

The church is called to exercise dominion on the earth, and it is the appointed time to act and actually celebrate your Passover salvation. As we do this it is important to remember that after Israel celebrated the Passover in Egypt, they marched out of that physical land holding material goods and wealth headed for another physical land where they were to conquer and dwell. God says that what should and will happen in the hands of the celebrating church is "immeasurably more than all we ask or imagine, according to his power that is at work within us" (Eph. 3:20).

Believers moving in the presence of God can and should affect virtually every aspect of their world. Being spiritual should not be limited to the worship service but should be demonstrated in successfully working, living, and being the most blessed people in every dimension of godly life on earth.

It is an essential step to entering the promised land life that God's army be a celebrating people prepared to march into the promises and the fulfillment of time for which we have been born to live. We must live our salvation fully and walk out our destiny completely. There is no other time like this time. God's people should celebrate the freedom that they have been given in Christ. You have an anointing that gives you and others life, deliverance, blessing, and prosperity. Now is the time to celebrate the tremendous liberty and freedom and power of God's life in you. Real faith will produce in believers an attitude of joyful praise, thanksgiving, celebration, and expectation of an immense future and an awareness of the total awesomeness of God that will propel the church forward into the greater works Jesus said we would do and the people the Word says we're to be.

CHAPTER 17

STEP#8 - MAKE
TWO TRUMPETS

The LORD said to Moses: "Make *two trumpets of hammered silver*, and use them for calling the community together and for having the camps set out. . . . When you go into battle in your own land against an enemy who is oppressing you, sound a blast on the trumpets. Then you will be remembered by the LORD your God and rescued from your enemies. Also at your times of rejoicing—your appointed festivals and New Moon feasts—you are to sound the trumpets over your burnt offerings and fellowship offerings, and they will be a memorial for you before your God. I am the LORD your God." (Numbers 10:1–2, 9–10, NIV)

The *eighth and final step of preparation* in the book of Numbers is the unique command to Moses to make *two trumpets of hammered silver.* The Israelites were certainly familiar with trumpets being used to signal them. However the kind of trumpet used up until now was the shofar or ram's horn. The Bible says:

> On the morning of the third day there was thunder and lightning, with a thick cloud over the mountain, and a very loud **trumpet** blast. Everyone in the camp trembled. Then Moses led the people out of the camp to meet with God, and they stood at the foot of the mountain. Mount Sinai was covered with smoke, because the LORD descended on it in fire. The smoke billowed up from it like smoke from a furnace, the whole mountain trembled violently, and the sound of the trumpet grew louder and louder. Then Moses spoke and the voice of God answered him." (Exodus 19:16–19, NIV)

It so happens that the word *trumpet* in these verses is the word *shofar* in Hebrew. This obviously is a supernatural event and the sounding of a supernatural trumpet. The Bible doesn't say who blew this shofar—maybe the Lord himself—but it was loud and served to signal the people to gather at Mount Sinai to meet with God. God later instructed the people to use this kind of trumpet in the celebrations of their feasts and for signaling troops in the midst of warfare.

The shofar could sound more than one pitch, but it was not intended as a musical instrument but a signaling instrument. It called people to gather, to be alarmed, to act or respond in some manner. The shofar harkens back to the time of Abraham and his worship on the mountain with Isaac. When Abraham was about to sacrifice Isaac on the altar to God, an angel stopped him, and Abraham saw a ram caught in a thicket by his horn. "Abraham looked up and there in a thicket he saw a ram caught by its horns. He went over and took the ram and sacrificed it as a burnt offering instead of his son. So Abraham called that place The LORD Will Provide. And to this day it is said, '*On the mountain of the LORD it will be provided*' " (Gen. 22:13–14, NIV, emphasis mine). Tradition says that this mount was Moriah, the same location of Solomon's Temple and the threshing floor purchased by David, his father.

It would seem that one thing we can gather from this event is that whenever the ram's horn is sounded, it should be a clear and loud reminder to the people of God that the Lord will provide. Sounding the shofar is like trumpeting the name Jehovah Jireh (the Lord will provide) and a call to faith in the God of provision, a clear call to assemble around the Lord in faith and to trust in the fullness of His promises. The shofar also is like a blaring declaration that sounds clearly in the face of the devil that God's promised ultimate provision, which was then yet to come, has now come in the person of Christ. Its sound is a reminder of the devil's defeat and that Christ has conquered and is conquering now.

THE NUMBER TWO

As powerful and meaningful as the blowing of the shofar was
then and is for the believer today, there would seem to be something even more significant and prophetically meaningful to
us in the unique command given to Moses to make two silver
trumpets. There is an added weight of significance in that this
is the final point of preparation before the Israelites left Sinai
and headed for the promised land. The Israelites were familiar
with the ram's horn, but this command was for a different kind
of trumpet, one hammered out of silver. Not only was the kind
of metal specified but also the exact number of instruments
was indicated: two.

The number two has its own significance for the Bible
student. Traditionally, the number two has been understood to
be the number of testimony or confirming witness. For example,
in the Old Testament we read that "on the testimony of two or
three witnesses a man shall be put to death, but no one shall be
put to death on the testimony of only one witness" (Deut. 17:6,
NIV). In the New Testament we read that when we confront a
brother in sin " if he will not listen, take one or two others along,
so that 'every matter may be established by the testimony of two
or three witnesses' " (Matt. 18:16, NIV). And Paul wrote: "This
will be my third visit to you. 'Every matter must be established
by the testimony of two or three witnesses' " (2 Cor. 13:1, NIV).

There are other Scriptures that affirm the requirement of at least two people when it came to testifying or establishing the truth of matters. In this way it would never be one individual's word against another individual but two or more eyewitnesses would be able to assure an accurate account of the truth.

The truth is important to God and is also essential to the establishment of kingdom living. Truth is the means of bringing God's freedom in life and how to live in the way and blessing of God. Evidently this was in the mind of God when it came time to tell the world the truth about the gospel of the kingdom for Jesus sent his disciples out in pairs ahead of himself: "After this the Lord appointed seventy-two others and sent them two by two ahead of him to every town and place where he was about to go" (Luke 10:1, NIV). The Lord followed His own command, of course, and made sure an adequate witness was given to the truth they carried. Each could testify to what they had seen, heard, and experienced in the ministry of Jesus.

Not only was the establishing of truth accomplished by two or more witnesses, but there is also a connection between the act of agreement of two with the manifestation of the presence and power of God. This is evident in Scripture: "Again, I tell you that if two of you on earth agree about anything you ask for, it will be done for you by my Father in heaven. For where two or three come together in my name, there am I with them" (Matt. 18:19–20, NIV). It would seem that with the establish-ment of God's truth and a firm agreement between two or more that God comes into the picture and confirms, by supernatural action, the validity of that truth Himself.

Agreeing with God's truth, believing His Word, and living in faithfulness is the way we advance His kingdom into this world. When you agree with God and obey His Word, you confirm His authority and power, and establish those unified in Him and in His purpose and truth.

THE TWO BECOME ONE

It is for this reason the picture of two becoming one is epitomized in the marriage union. The apostle Paul quotes Christ who was quoting the Old Testament and then added an explanation when he said, " 'For this reason a man will leave his father and mother and be united to his wife, and the two will become one flesh.' This is a profound mystery—but I am talking about Christ and the church" (Eph. 5:31–32, NIV). Here Paul is using the union of a man and woman in marriage to illustrate the love and power intended for the union of Christ and the church. The picture is of a joining together of two into one and as such the creation of a new life and a new way of life that is the goal of God for His people.

This same imagery of union is used with relationship between the gentiles and the Jews and what Christ is to accomplish between them:

Therefore, remember that formerly you who are Gentiles by birth and called "uncircumcised" by those who call themselves "the circumcision" (that done in the body by the hands of men)—remember that at that time you were separate from Christ, excluded from citizenship in Israel and foreigners to the covenants of the promise, without hope and without God in the world. But now in Christ Jesus you who once were far away have been brought near through the blood of Christ. For he himself is our peace, who has *made the two one* and has destroyed the barrier, the dividing wall of hostility, by abolishing in his flesh the law with its commandments and regulations. His purpose was to create in himself *one new man out of the two*, thus making peace," (Ephesians 2:11–15, NIV, emphasis mine)

Notice that God's stated purpose is the creation of *one new man out of two*. That *one* new man would then live in agreement with God and maintain oneness with each other by being in Christ and being the body of believers in the earth today.

THE TWO SILVER TRUMPETS

Is it possible that the Lord had in mind something far more powerful and glorious than the church has imagined when he speaks of "one new man out of two"? Remember that the two trumpets were to be constructed of silver. Traditionally, silver, being a precious metal, would represent the redemption of Christ. The thirty pieces of silver paid to Judas was the price for his betrayal of Christ. Not only was the material to be silver, but it was also to be beaten. Again this represents the abuse that Christ suffered for our redemption. Putting these several types or prophetic images together we have a picture of two witnesses, Jew and gentile, confirming the truth that reflects the power and high cost of redemption.

We have already looked at Paul's word to the Ephesians revealing God's plan to make one new man out of two, meaning the joining of Jew and gentile together in Christ. Paul also brings up another point concerning the Jews in his letter to Rome. Paul says, "For if their rejection brought reconciliation of the world, what will their acceptance be but life from the dead?" (Rom. 11:15, NIV). Paul seems to indicate a significant and pivotal event yet to be seen in all its fullness when he speaks of "life from the dead." Life from the dead is just another way of saying revival or being revived to life. He also speaks of the gentile believers having the capacity to evoke envy in the Jews: "Again I ask: Did they stumble so as to fall beyond recovery? Not at all! Rather, because of their transgression, salvation has come to the gentiles to make Israel envious" (Rom. 11:11, NIV).

The implication is that at some time yet in the future Jews provoked by the believing body of gentiles would turn to their

Redeemer. The gentile church is to be the stimulus that will bring about a resurrection of life in Israel. This revival of the Jews to new life in Yeshua, their Messiah, will produce *two witnesses* to the world. It is these two groups, Jew and gentile that the two trumpets of Numbers point to. It is these two witnesses that need to sound their clear and powerful call to rally the people of God to advance into the true promised land of God.

A CLEAR SOUND

Paul, in writing the Corinthians asks a reasonable question: "Again, if the trumpet does not sound a clear call, who will get ready for battle?" (1 Cor. 14:8, NIV). A clear call or a discernible sound is necessary to succeed in the purpose for which the trumpet was created. The sound of the gospel trumpet sounded by the traditional and current church has been too unclear and has not served to truly rally the people or move them to action. The sound that has come forth is one of individual salvation and heavenly orientation rather than a call to advance kingdom and covenant living here on earth. The church is often full of worldly confusion and a distorted vision concerning the purpose and plan of God for His people. A plan to have a people filled with His presence with power to conquer enemies and to deliver people as He prospers their lives in every way.

Interestingly, Christians are often concerned about the sins of unbelievers in the world and fear God judging the world because of that sin. But the Bible says, "it is time for judgment to begin with the family of God" (1 Pet. 4:17). God starts his judgments with His people first. People in the church should be far more concerned about the sins Christians are committing than what is happening in the world.

The world will always sin. But the church must confront its own sins of apathy towards the things of God, disobedience, dishonor of authority, and the greatest sin of all, unbelief. Many today do not believe in the power of God to accomplish His plan and will. This is far worse than sin in the world; we should expect sin in the world but not in God's house. I'm not talking about an expectation of perfection or sinlessness but about shedding the expectation of sin and a destiny of weakness. The church should have the expectation of being like Christ and walking in godliness by His power.

God is waiting to see people of faith rise up, just like He did with Israel of old in the wilderness. He is looking for a Joshua generation to believe Him and act on His Word. God is planning on Jew and gentile coming together in faith and proclaiming the truth of God's kingdom. When these two redeemed segments of God's people come together like a clear and unified voice sounding the true good news of God's kingdom to the world and living like true kingdom people, then something great and awesome will transpire. The two trumpets were not to sound different pitches but were to play in unison and sound the same note, making it both louder and clearer and more able to pierce through the din of religious noise filling the worldly battlefield with confusion, carnality, and unbelief. The sound of these trumpets is to prepare God's people to be ready for battle, to conquer the promised land.

The command in Numbers 10 was the eighth and final command given to Moses, and it was to prepare Israel to enter and conquer the promised land. Eight is considered by many to be the number of new beginning. Entering the land God promised was to be a new start for God's covenant people, a new land and a new way of living for them. But they couldn't just walk in. They were going to have to battle for that which had been promised to them. The believer today must expect the same thing but with an even greater expectation of victory.

GOD REMEMBERS

In the text I quoted at the beginning of this chapter there is an additional promise and command to them:

> When you go into battle in your own land against an enemy who is oppressing you, sound a blast on the trumpets. Then *you will be remembered by the LORD* your God and rescued from your enemies. Also at your times of rejoicing—your appointed festivals and New Moon feasts—you are to sound the trumpets over your burnt offerings and fellowship

offerings, and they will be a memorial for you before your God. I am the LORD your God." (Numbers 10:9–10, NIV)

Any time God starts talking about a memorial or about remembering Him, He is thinking about action not just fond memories. The terms *be remembered* or *bring to remembrance* when referring to God mean bring Him to action. He thinks, perceives, and is brought to action. Paul quotes Jesus in his letter to the Corinthians: "In the same way, after supper he took the cup, saying, 'This cup is the new covenant in my blood; do this, whenever you drink it, in remembrance of me.' " (1 Corinthians 11:25, NIV).

When Jesus said to do something "in remembrance of me," it was meant to bring you not only to awareness but to action. It is supposed to activate faith in you that motivates you to respond to God's will. For example, as we've said before, when taking Communion or celebrating the Passover, the believer should not just think back to a past historic happening but come alive to a present and living power and reality working actively in them now. Believers are to be changed people living changed lives and affecting the world around them like an invading army conquers and transforms the land of its' enemy.

THE ULTIMATE ACTION

Those trumpets were to be sounded to gather the people, to direct and move the people to action, to warn the people and to be a part of their rejoicing. God isn't interested in stirring memories but in motivating and moving His people to action and victory. Notice it was when the army went into battle and sounded the trumpets that God said He would respond and act on their behalf and rescue them from their enemies. God requires His people to be entering and conquering the promised land and not sitting around reminiscing about past glories. God wants two silver trumpets, a type representing the Jews and the gentiles, sounding together the proclamation of the Word of God, in the anointing of God, as the one people of God moving in the promises of God.

The ultimate fulfillment of what we are talking about today, the empowering of the whole of God's people to impact the entire world, is waiting for the Jew to come into the fullness of the covenant. Unfortunately, many in the church are convinced, having been taught by some teachers of end time events, that there is a very dark and terrible time coming for the Jews to endure and the church will already been taken out of the world, so it will not be around to help the Jews, much less make them envious (Rom. 11:11). There are prophetic texts that indicate there will be a great conflagration or battle in the end of this age, but before that takes place there is much to be done to prepare the bride of Christ to be presented to the Bridegroom and the Jews are to be part of that bride.

As the true body, the believers and followers of Jesus Christ including both Jew and gentile, begin to march forward working and battling together, the kingdom of God will advance into the fullest expression of life it has ever had

CHAPTER 18

GOD'S PRESENCE CONQUERS

Now when Balaam saw that it pleased the LORD to bless Israel, he did not resort to sorcery as at other times, but turned his face toward the desert. When Balaam looked out and saw Israel encamped tribe by tribe, the Spirit of God came upon him and he uttered his oracle: "The oracle of Balaam son of Beor, the oracle of one whose eye sees clearly, the oracle of one who hears the words of God, who sees a vision from the Almighty, who falls prostrate, and whose eyes are opened: "How beautiful are your tents, O Jacob, your dwelling places, O Israel! "Like valleys they spread out, like gardens beside a river, like aloes planted by the LORD, like cedars beside the waters. Water will flow from their buckets; their seed will have abundant water. "Their king will be greater than Agag;

their kingdom will be exalted. "God brought them out of Egypt; they have the strength of a wild ox. They devour hostile nations and break their bones in pieces; with their arrows they pierce them. Like a lion they crouch and lie down, like a lioness—who dares to rouse them? "May those who bless you be blessed and those who curse you be cursed!" (Numbers 24:1–9)

To finish the revelation of God's kingdom advance, let's look at a summary event that occurs in Numbers chapter twenty-four. A Moabite man named Balaam had a reputation as a prophet able to hear from God and prophesy. Balaam, because of his reputation is hired by a Moabite king named Balak to curse Israel. Balak was afraid Israel would conquer his nation and lands. Balak foolishly thought that Balaam could use his spiritual gift to proclaim or invoke a curse against Israel so they would lose the blessing of God. To apply this event to our lives today we need to understand from this story that the rulers, powers, and spiritual authorities of the kingdoms of this world are just as afraid of the people of God today, if not even more so, as Balak was afraid of Israel then.

THE BEAUTY OF GOD'S PEOPLE

In verse 1 of the text, Balaam looks out over the valley and he sees the camped army of the Israelites. It is important to note that it was the *faithful, disciplined and assembled camp, gathered in community tribe by tribe*, that he saw. When Balaam looked at their encampment, he was so overwhelmed by what he saw *he couldn't curse them; he could only bless them*. The lesson is that when the church is assembled and functioning in as the body of Christ, worshipping together and prepared to be the army of Christ, men will not curse the church; they will bless the church and even come into life with the church.

The unity and communion of God in His house will bring victory over the enemies of God. Currently, the carnality, disunity, confusion, and mixed messages that the church has presented to those we want to impress is not a pretty picture. The general church image is not beautiful, but a hypocritical thing that brings the image of a curse upon it. This is changing and the body of Christ is not going to stay that way, and when we walk in faith, a worshipping people, and under authority, the curse will be turned back. The church is destined to be a blessing, and God will be pleased to bless us and then neither the world nor the devil will ever be able to overcome or stop the church from the dominion and kingdom life it should have.

There was something so beautiful and godly about just the appearance of the camp of Israel that Balaam's words turned to blessing instead of cursing. We, the church, bring much cursing upon ourselves from the mouths of men, but it is not for being godly or righteous but for being unchristlike, unwise, powerless, and self-defeating. In describing the church as a bride, the Bible says, "Let us rejoice and be glad and give him glory! For the wedding of the Lamb has come, and his bride has made herself ready. Fine linen, bright and clean, was given her to wear" (Rev. 19:7–8, NIV). It says the bride has made herself ready and was given fine linen to wear. The linen is defined as the "righteous acts of the saints."

That means believers, living and not dead, did things or acted righteously. One of the best ways to think of righteous behavior is as godlike behavior. The actions of the church should be godlike in character and nature. The church should manifest a character or image like that of Jesus when he walked the earth, healing, delivering, blessing, manifesting power over the devil, confronting hypocrisy, and demonstrating joy, faith and love.

The truth of the gospel of the kingdom, when it is preached in context and with anointing, will produce power, prosperity, and life transformation wherever it is presented and faithfully walked out. When the church learns to walk in agreement as one new man with one sound, then no curse will succeed against it. The church walking together in the Spirit of Christ has the power to be like Him in this world and defeat all its enemies, and redeem the land, the entire earth, for the kingdom of God.

VICTORY AND NOT DEFEAT

One final biblical picture that points to the victory of the church occurs in Revelation:

After that I saw heaven opened, and behold, a white horse [appeared], and He who was riding it is called Faithful and True (trustworthy, loyal, incorruptible, steady), and in righteousness *He judges and wages war [on the rebellious nations]*. His eyes are a flame of fire, and on His head are many royal crowns; and He has a name inscribed [on Him] which no one knows or understands except Himself. He is dressed in a robe dipped in blood, and His name is called The Word of God. And the armies *of heaven, dressed in fine linen, [dazzling] white and clean*, followed Him on white horses. From His mouth comes a sharp sword (His word) with which He may strike down the nations, and *He will rule them* with a rod of iron. He will tread the winepress of the fierce wrath of God, the Almighty [in judgment of the rebellious world]. And on His robe and on His thigh He has a name inscribed, KING OF KINGS AND LORD OF LORDS. " (Revelation 19:11-16, AMP, emphasis mine)

Read these verses again carefully and ask yourself what John was trying to express to the church in his day with these words. I know some think these verses are about Jesus when

He comes back at the end of everything to rescue the poor, desperate, hanging on church. Let me challenge you to change your thinking and consider that these verses are not about Him coming back to rescue the church, but it is a picture of Him moving out in battle formation right now with His church.

Can you see that it is happening now and is a spiritual picture of the Lord Jesus going out into the earth to exact war against evil and iniquity through the church. Believers are the instruments He will use to bring judgment and defeat to evil and iniquity while bringing justice to bear in His name and His authority. Notice it says, "He will shepherd them." Jesus is the great Shepherd, and He wants to move out into the darkness of this earth and actually rule in righteousness.

The church has the power to overwhelm and defeat wickedness. Remember Jesus said "all authority" had been given to Him. Ask yourself what's the best way to defeat sin and a sinner? The answer is to cause them to know the true King and kingdom of God. You should think of God's warfare in terms of changing people not necessarily removing people. When individuals become His disciples, they cease being an enemy and remove themselves by dying to self. Real disciples are called to crucify themselves. This is true spiritual imagery for the conquering gospel of the kingdom that reaps victory in the earth. Let's have a bigger image of Gods plan. As His kingdom expands His people are to become the dominant people because our first mandate was a "dominion mandate."

The second mandate was "go and make disciples of all nations" (Matt. 28:19). This also fulfills the dominion mandate because once people become His disciples, they are following Him and not the devil. The devil begins losing more and more of his disciples; he becomes a truly defeated and beaten foe, a mere shadow of what he was. Then his final judgment can come, and he will be assigned to the fires of hell. But the plan is that there will be a victorious church before that time.

Some have taught a different eschatology (end time picture) that quite frankly is counter to the purpose of God. There are whole series of books, thousands of recordings and online downloads and websites that can cause Christians to be overcome by fear and expect the rise of evil and wickedness in the world to such an extent that it would be more successful than the people of God. The issue isn't whether evil things will come, for they will, but the issue is who has the authority and power to ultimately overcome and be victorious in the end.

Telling the church today that it has been given a mandate to overcome the evil of this world and expand the kingdom of God into that world could make one feel a lot like Joshua and Caleb must have felt when they were trying to convince Israel to believe God and go in and take the land:

Joshua son of Nun and Caleb son of Jephunneh, who were among those who had explored the land, tore their clothes and said to the entire Israelite assembly, "The land we passed through and explored is exceedingly good. If the Lord is pleased with us, he will lead us into that land, a land flowing with milk and honey, and will give it to us. Only do not rebel against the Lord. And do not be afraid of the people of the land, because we will swallow them up. Their protection is gone, but the Lord is with us. Do not be afraid of them." (Numbers 14:6–9)

They were shouted down by the unbelieving people, and unbelief ruled. Israel had been only a few days travel away from the fullness of what God desired for them but ended up struggling in the wilderness for forty years. They wandered in the wilderness of unbelief until that generation died off and faith lived and ruled.

You can look around and see the evil that is happening in our world. The world is so humanistic, materialistic, and disinterested in the true God, and maybe some of what we call the church is exactly the same way. But I hear God roaring like he did in the days of Elijah:

Then he said to me, "Prophesy to these bones and say to them, 'Dry bones, hear the word of the LORD! This is what the Sovereign LORD says to these bones: I will make breath enter you, and you will come to life. I will attach tendons to you and make flesh come upon you and cover you with skin; I will put breath in you, and you will come to life. Then you will know that I am the LORD.' " So I prophesied as I was commanded. And as I was prophesying, there was a noise, a rattling sound, and the bones came together, bone to bone. I looked, and tendons and flesh appeared on them and skin covered them, but there was no breath in them. Then he said to me, "Prophesy to the breath; prophesy, son of man, and say to it, 'This is what the Sovereign LORD says: Come from the four winds, O breath, and breathe into these slain, that they may live.' " So I prophesied as he commanded me, and breath entered them; they came to life and stood up on their feet—a vast army. (Ezekiel 37:4–10)

There is a prophetic sound of the Spirit today.

We must stop our doubting and fear. God is speaking today like He did to Joshua: "The LORD gave this command to Joshua son of Nun: "Be strong and courageous, for you will bring the Israelites into the land I promised them on oath, and I myself will be with you" (Deut. 31:23). We can then say like Elisha,

" 'Don't be afraid,' the prophet answered. *'Those who are with us are more than those who are with them'* " (2 Kings 6:16, emphasis mine).

God expects the church to rise up and honor the authority it has been given. It is the plan of God for the mandates He has decreed to be fulfilled, and He is in the process of expanding and increasing the establishment of His kingdom in all the earth. This is the day of the forceful kingdom of God fulfilling its promises.

It is time for the people of God to conquer the promised land: of themselves and the unbelieving world as well. Believers are to live in the true kingdom life and faithfully steward everything by God's principles. As they do this, they will be soldiers and serve as helpers throughout all the earth. Kingdom people will overcome unbelief and vain religion by living a victorious and overcoming life in Christ as His spiritually militant and advancing church. God wants a church marching forward in the truth and power of His Spirit. A people standing on the promises of His Word and exercising the authority God has given and progressively and powerfully establishing His will in the earth as in heaven. A people filled with the worship of their God.

There are two trumpets being created to sound together the call to assemble and conquer the promised land. The choice is ours to obey, to advance by living as kingdom people in the earth today, walking in the presence of God. God has given a plan to be believed and followed. As believers we must not limit God or doubt His desire and ability to do miraculous works in us. He will build His church and see His plan fulfilled.

The steps God gave Israel in Numbers are valid for us today. While I'm certain there were other issues the leaders and people had to deal with as they moved toward the promised land, these eight steps given Moses were essential to what God wanted to accomplish in Israel. If we will seek God's help to apply and follow those steps today, then we can enter into the spiritual promised land of God of this earth. Joshua and Caleb finally moved Israel forward when the people had faith to move together and followed the steps to fulfillment. The God we worship and give ourselves to does not fail. To those in Christ we say: follow the steps as His body, hear the sound and call, be bold, advance and conquer the promised land! "The kingdom of the world has become the kingdom of our LORD and of his Christ, and he will reign for ever and ever" (Rev. 11:15). Amen!

Made in the USA
Las Vegas, NV
23 August 2021